The POWER *of* RELEASING JUDGMENT

Editor
ERICA GLESSING

Happy Publishing

EXPONENTIALIZE HAPPINESS

Daria Hanson

Are you looking for a deeper happiness in your life? Are you aware that one of the gifts you can give yourself to exponentialize happiness in your life – with ease – is to release judgment? What do I mean?

We have been entrained to believe that if we get it right, our life will finally work out and we will be happy. So you spend every moment of your life trying to get the right judgment in life... the right grades, right body, right relationships, right career, right success, right answers. If that were true, wouldn't your life be a paradise by now? I know how much time you have spent and how much energy you have invested in getting your life right. I have been there, done that! But instead, are you finding yourself in the constant search for the next right judgment, in hope that if you would get enough of "right" in your life, you would finally be able to break this cycle of "never being enough" and finally being happy with yourself and able to enjoy the rest of your life?

What if a secret to the end of the self-judgment

cycle and the start of happiness is vulnerability?

What if vulnerability is the source of creation of your life? What if running around with your head down making sure you reach your next right place is just maintaining your existence, rather than creating your life? I have learned in my life that it is impossible to create your life in search for right. Life as you desire it to be can only be created from a space of total vulnerability, a space of total receiving that is impossible if you hold on to any judgment. Nothing that does not match your judgment will be able to enter your world. So if you have been asking for a different life, to be happy, to be self-content and you have not been able to reach that yet, it is probably because you have a certain judgment that you have acquired throughout your life that keeps that which you are asking for away. But if you release that judgment, everything becomes possible.

Let's let go of the rightness, as where rightness is, judgment exists.

We hope that this book could be an opening to a new possibility for you to choose to go beyond judgment, beyond rightness, and simply embrace that which you know you would like to create your life as and enjoy the journey with the tools and techniques that this book is rich in.

Daria

TABLE OF CONTENTS

CHAPTER 1

SPACE OF BEING

Bettina Madini

"Oh, the Beauty of the Earth!
Receive it, my friends, for it is for you, always!
In the fractions between your thoughts.
Make that real which inspires you,
not that which puts you down.
Keep the intensity of the rainbow
and the setting sun in your recalling,
and thoughts and sorrow will vanish
With the laughter."

~ Bettina

Invitation

When I received the invitation for contributing a chapter to this book I happily replied with a joyful yes! It was so light and expansive. Once I opened my laptop and sat in front of the empty page I wasn't quite sure where to even begin. Judgment, I wondered, was everywhere. How could I approach something so vast, so slippery and multi-faceted in one chapter? How could I approach something that is the very core and structure of this entire reality, in a few pages?

So, let me invite you on a walk, on a journey. I have no idea where we will be going. There are so many possibilities as to how this journey could unfold. So, let's go sit by a tree.

A tree will not judge you, nature overall does not judge you. Have you noticed? The sense of ease and relaxation in nature is created by the total lack of judgment.

Where judgment stops is where being begins

Being is not something that we have to become or find, or something outside of us. We are that already. It just got obstructed and diminished. We all allowed judgment to be more real than choosing for us.

The space of being is a space that does not know judgment. Being is when we express our joy and choose what we would like to create. It is the space where we honor ourselves, and others. We don't change ourselves for others, nor do we cut off pieces of ourselves so that others will like us. We don't blindly succumb to tradition or follow in anybody's footsteps without asking questions. It is the space beyond definition, beyond roles and confinement. We include everything and everyone in our choices, also the earth and also our bodies. We are totally present and live from question and awareness, curiosity and the willingness to change.

What if we never judged anyone or anything, not even ourselves, not even our bodies?

This reality that we think is real

I grew up in Berlin in the 1960s, a time marked by separation and cold war. Who could come up with the idea of separating a city by building a wall right through it, with both parts being governed by different political points of view and social systems, each part based on the assumption that they were 'right'?

The trees stand still. Turmoil of human creation will not disturb their being. They stand and wait, for us to choose something different.

My family was on the West side, and I grew up with all the amenities of Western culture. As a child, I couldn't understand the concept of the wall. There was no space in my universe for long waiting and seemingly endless controls at borders, military police with guns, and a strange energy of fear that was hanging like a thick cloak above the long, trailing lines of silent cars waiting at the check point, an inevitable procedure on the way to vacation destinations.

In all these strange dynamics of human creation, I had my own small oasis in the middle of the city. My grandparents had a garden in

Berlin. I spent half of my waking days there, a happy child when I could be by fruit trees, flowers, berries and garden beds. I would plant seeds, pick cherries and watch nature from soft blankets in the shade.

Do you get the insanity of judgment? Do you see the creations that we choose when we judge?

Any judgment, whether we consider something as right or wrong, whether we think something is great or horrible, creates a limitation. Judgments, definitions and conclusions are everywhere. Just turn on the news.

If we had no judgments, would we have a different world?

Now, this is what interests me. If we had no judgment, what would be possible? If we didn't judge ourselves what could we create? If there was no right and wrong, could there be walls?

How much do we limit ourselves with judgments? When we think we have to do things a certain way, 'the right way', we create the very limit of our own reality, the wall that we cannot overcome, and we drain our being. For every judgment, there are many other judgments that hold that one judgment in place. It is like a multi-level structure. Judgments become the walls that separate us from our being, our body and the earth.

You know somewhere within you that something different is possible. Otherwise, you wouldn't be here, reading this book. You might have wondered what different reality was possible, a reality that was not based on judgment but built upon allowance?

Are you a dreamer? Can you imagine a world based on joy and happiness, respect and allowance? A reality that also includes the earth? Not just from a scientific point of view, but based on caring for the living being that we call the earth?

We live in a world that is basically made of judgment. Judgment is the positive as well as the negative.

We all know negative judgment, and we avoid it by all means. We want people to like us, we want to belong, we want to 'get along'. How much judgment does all that require? Without even being aware of it, we spend huge amounts of our energy evaluating others, and ourselves, we judge constantly and incessantly. Like fine-tuned antennas, we use our senses to measure and evaluate, and we don't even recognize it. Then, we cut off pieces and parts of ourselves, those pieces that we censored 'unacceptable' about ourselves, or 'not good enough'.

Our mind collects data, analyzes, compares with the past and interprets, constantly. We agree with others or we resist and fight them, we conclude that we like them or don't like them. Instead of judging and excluding, we could just simply choose not to live with them.

What if instead of judging we made a choice? Would that be easier? And what does this even mean, you might wonder?

Judgment is when we put up barriers and we separate.

The interesting thing is that judgment is not only the negative. Positive judgment is even trickier, as we easily accept it and we don't catch it as judgment. Have you ever noticed, when someone compliments you on the suit you are wearing or your new dress and then, you find yourself wearing it a lot? Would that positive judgment have created a limitation? Yes. If we make it significant. Each time we are looking for validation, do we actually see our value? No. When we search something outside of us, we have decided already that it is not in us, so we must find it outside of us.

What would it take to change this? And, is this all even real?

Judgment as the wall that defines our box

We use judgments to define who we are and what we can or cannot choose and be.

While I was still living in Luxemburg, I took evening classes at the 'Ecole d'art Contemporain', after work. I greatly enjoyed painting there on weekday evenings and very often also on Saturdays. I proudly had labeled myself as 'abstract artist'. I enjoyed experimenting with colors, and I made sure that no figurative shape would show up on my canvas.

I was in control of things, at least so I thought. One sunny afternoon, these beings showed up in the blue world that I was painting. I didn't know what to do with them! I totally resisted and even fought them, and I was so upset that I wanted to destroy the canvas. I went into an angry lament for about a week. Luckily, I knew that there was something for me to look at. I knew that the painting was showing me something that I had been unwilling to see and receive before. So, I stayed with my upset, and after a week, I lightened up. Out of the blue, I had the idea to take drawing classes and study figure, something that I had not even considered before. Oh, my universe opened up! There was such a lightness and joy. I started right away in Luxembourg, and continued in New York City, where I emerged myself into studying figure and portrait. This was so much fun! Pretty soon, I discovered that I had great ease with it and that I could draw anything! I had gone around a wall that I had created to limit me.

With defining myself as an abstract artist, I had stuck myself into polarity, the good and the bad. Abstract was good, form and shape were bad. With that definition, did I choose to be unlimited or limited? Did I have infinite choice with my creations, or finite choice? Finite choice. I had literally created a box that would limit what I could paint. I had to judge each painting as to whether it was 'right or wrong' and whether it would fit into my definition.

What if we never defined ourselves? Would we have more choice?

Are you judging you?
Are you judging your body?

In a world built upon a structure of judgment, it is easy to follow in the footsteps of
everyone around us, and society entirely. We actually learn to use judgment so we can fit in, so we can 'function' in life. Have you ever noticed how much energy it takes to judge? With every judgment, we place another brick onto our wall, and pretty soon, all we can see is the wall.

Growing up I learned 'the way we do things' in my family and I was entrained with these pathways. Yet, there was something in me, a yearning for more, a desire to create greater and not copy what everyone else was doing. There was a powerful engine in me that fueled a thirst for a different reality, a happier reality! I could not accept the box that I was shown everywhere around me, as all there is! I knew something different was possible.

It was not until 2003 that I shifted my life,

moved to a different country and, this time around, also changed continents. I moved to New York City and continued my art education. This was my dream, to live as artist, to create whatever I desired to create as my life.

I sold my belongings, emptied a house full of collected pieces, furniture and family treasures. Everything had to go and find new owners, except for a few things that I kept. For two weeks, I watched my former belongings walk out of the house, one by one, finding new homes in my neighborhood. There was great beauty in that release. My neighbors were beaming with joy over the great finds that they carried away with them. And what space did it create in my universe!

I was full of excitement and the sense of adventure, and, yes, what adventure did I create! I had unprecedented bumps in the road, broken promises and a lot of unexpected change. Yet I knew that, whatever would come my way, I would be ok. My grandfather had always told us to "Never look back!" and I never did.

With enthusiasm and curiosity I danced into a new chapter of my life. It was a big change, and for the first several weeks, I was busy finding an art school and signing up for classes. The school I chose had a Bohemian flair. The air carried the energy of so many artists walking the hallways before me, exploring color, searching on their creative journeys, for the one brushstroke that would birth a creation into the world, at the first tickles of dawn. There, I emerged myself into study, joy and vulnerability.

Is there judgment in the art world? Oh, yes! It's called 'critique'. This world even suggests that an artist has to be critical to achieve 'their best'. Is it really true that the critical, constant thought process of the mind CAN inspire something new and lead us to thriving heights of possibility? Or, is the space of 'no thought' a richer, more fertile ground for possibility, inspiration and joy? What is possible when we are free from any point of view and we allow the universe to play with us? Does this sound too easy?

What ease can we have if we don't judge? Would you be willing to choose ease?

How do we get beyond judgment? And, what is the space of being?

Our minds are calculating systems that use judgment to evaluate, measure, compare and conclude. If you observe your mind well, you will find that it usually relates to and refers to the past. When you face a 'problem', no matter whether in your job or with your family, or with money, your mind will pull up information from the past, like a filing cabinet, and compare and come up with solutions, which are answers. It will usually not bring up something totally new.

When you had your most recent 'inspired' moment or brilliant idea, did this inspiration or idea, come out of a lengthy thought process? Or did it 'fly in' out of the blue, when you were not thinking?

When I paint, I don't think. I don't do composition, cognitively. It all unfolds with ease, and there is no effort. I don't think for hours before I make the next brush stroke. I rather follow the energy. Even if sometimes the flow slows down, I don't judge it. I know that this is part of the creation.

Instead of judging, I will ask a question. I ask the painting "Are you done?" Are you ready to go out into the world?" Sometimes, I'm getting a 'Yes!' At other times, the energy will pick up again and I will continue painting, I might even walk away from the painting for longer periods, knowing that somewhere I might see a color or a shape that will invite another motion for my painting. It is not logical, and it doesn't make sense. 'Making sense' is also judgment. And who is the judge?

Would you be willing to not make sense?

Create a judgment-free zone for you

Being so used to judgment on a day-to-day basis and having lived in a judgment-based reality for however long, you might wonder by now how to get out of judgment. A great way to start is for you to experience an environment where there is no judgment, where you can just 'be you'.

If you would like to be in a judgment-free zone, the best space to be is in nature. A forest does not judge you, a tree does not discourage you, a bird will not criticize your choices.

Have you noticed that when you are in nature that you relax, that your body relaxes? When you look at the ocean or you stand on a mountain and you enjoy the view, do you have thoughts? Or, is your head rather empty?

Nature doesn't judge you. Each tree appreciates your very being, is grateful for you just being in the world. Have you ever considered the earth being grateful for you?

What can we receive from the earth that we have never been willing to receive before?

Relaxation exercise with a tree

Would you be willing to spend half an hour with this exercise? Once a week, at least?

Go to your favorite tree. If you have a physical tree that you like to sit by, go there. If you don't, or if you live in an environment that doesn't allow for that, sit down on a comfortable pillow or sofa in your room. Make sure you have a moment of quiet, preferably a half an hour or so.

Remember what it was like, what you sensed in your body when you last sat by a tree. No matter how long ago, whether it was in this lifetime or a different lifetime. Whenever, wherever that was, recall that moment and get the sensation in your body of leaning against a tree.

Allow your mind to relax and let thoughts just float by. Deeply inhale and exhale. Get a sense of the space around you. Be aware of everything around you. Noise, an airplane, cars, people, the breeze, birds, other animals, the sounds of the forest or the ocean, wherever you are. Just be aware. Be aware of your body. Is there any pain or intensity in your body? Take deep inhales and long exhales and allow that pain or intensity to flow into the earth. Don't resist the pain. Just notice it and be present with it. Let it even get more intense. More. More. Yes. Now, let it flow out of your body. It is just energy that stopped moving. Move it out of your body. What if that was an energy that the earth can use? Let it flow, let it move into the earth. And breathe. Be aware of the ground beneath you.

Feel the tree having your back. Notice the tree trunk holding you and lean and relax into that strong hold. If tears come up let them flow. If anger comes up, notice it in your body. Where is it located in your body? Let it flow into the earth. What if this energy could even be a contribution to the earth? What if you are a contribution to the earth? Let it flow.

Do you notice things shifting in your body? Does your body feel different? Do you have a different sensation in your body?

And now, relax even more. Take a deep inhale and a long exhale.

Allow all the judgment that you have about you to come up, here in the forest. Whatever it is in your life that you think you have not accomplished, everywhere you thought you're not good enough, everything you thought you did wrong, everywhere you thought you made a mistake or failed. Let it come up. Where you think you were not a good mother or father, sister or brother, wife or husband, everywhere you hold a grudge against yourself or someone else. All the judgment you have about your past, your family, your job, colleagues, etc. Let come up whatever desires to come to the surface, while here by the tree. Again, notice the strength of the tree trunk and being held by it. Place your hands on its roots and feel the bark, notice the soft moss. Let your being and body open up these areas where you have solidified judgment, where you have locked it in your body, and let it flow. You don't have to figure it out. You don't have to analyze it or find the reason. Just let it go. Feel the presence of the tree. The tree is not judging you. It is just there. Be totally present with you. If more tears come up, let them flow. Your body is releasing what you have been holding back for so long. Let it flow. Let all the judgment flow into the earth. Move it outside of you.

What if you have never done anything wrong? What if you are not wrong?

In the beginning there might be a lot coming up for you. There, by your tree, relax. You don't have to hold onto anything.

Allow yourself to be taken into the oceans of energy, flowing and breathing motion with your being that desires to shine in the world. Relax into where the tree and the earth are taking you, beyond of what you thought was possible. Gaze into the lights, beaming within the dark soil and golden roots, knowing that somewhere deep, deep down in the earth, there is a light; so warm and so bright that nothing, nothing can diminish it. The beauty that is there, has been there always, waiting patiently for your willingness to step into that ease that is so joy-filled and inspiring that it can move mountains, dissolve anger, judgment and fear and gently point ahead to the future that is more now than a shimmer. Beyond the treacherous concept of judgment is knowing, is your being.

From beneath the roots, from the dark warmth of our earth, rises a potent kindness that breathes nurturance and joy into your body and being. All this is here, my friends, for you to claim and own, and acknowledge in you. Would you be willing to receive THAT level of kindness and gratitude, and be it for you? The earth has desired to gift it to you for a long, long time. Yet can she not give you what you refuse. Are you willing to receive it NOW?

Breathe. Allow the energy to flow in. Relax. Stay here as long as you desire.

Once you notice that the intensity ceases, place your hands on your body and say "Thank you!" to your body. Notice the energy and warmth flowing from your hands to your body and from your body to your hands. Be with this gratitude, receive it and gift it. Let it flow both ways.

Now place your hands onto the tree trunk and say "Thank you, tree!" and let your energy flow to the tree while also receiving the energy of the tree. Place your hands onto the earth and say "Thank you, earth, for being here for me!" and let the energy flow both ways, from you to the earth and also from the earth to you.

Stay there leaning against the tree for as long as you wish. Be with the earth, with the tree, with all the beings of the forest that are showing up for you. Whatever energy is there and available for you, receive it. It might be a warmth, joy, exhilaration, it might be space or undefined energy. Just be with it, whatever it is.

What can you create from this space of no judgment?

Keep asking questions

Here by your tree, whether in the forest or in your backyard, or in the park, or wherever you are, from this space, from the ease and peace, do you get a sense of what your life could be like, if there was no judgment? What is the energy that you would like to have in your life?

And, what if you chose that? *Would you be willing to not judge you again, ever?*

Now that you got a sense of the space of no judgment, you can start creating a different reality for you, a reality that is based on kindness and allowance. Each time you notice judgment, let it go. A judgment is only a point of view. Ask "What else can I choose here?" and "If I didn't have a judgment now, what could I create?"

This will get easier with practice. Keep choosing! If you judge, it's a choice. Not to judge is also a choice. What do you choose?

You, the being, are everything. The more you release judgment, the more of you is going to show up in the world and the more you are going to receive that the universe has your back. That is the power of letting go of the lies of judgment.

Would you be willing to enter this journey? I cannot tell you what you are going to find, and I cannot promise you anything. Yet, what if today is the beginning of something so joyful, so exciting and inspiring that nobody *can* promise you *what* you will find, as this very promise would limit what you CAN discover?

About the Author

BETTINA MADINI

 Bettina Madini is an artist, singer and an Access Consciousness® Certified Facilitator.

She was born in Berlin, Germany. In 1992, she moved to Luxemburg and pursued a career in the corporate world. Bettina resumed her art education in 1998 in Luxemburg at the Ecole d'Art Contemporain and studied with Jean-Marc Tossello. In 2003, she moved to New York City, where she continued exploring art at the National Academy School of Fine Arts and studied with Susan Shatter, Sharon Sprung, Henry Finkelstein and Wolf Kahn. She has been living and working (or should we say 'playing'?) as a creative being in the United States since 2004.

Bettina loves to inspire the world to a different possibility, with everything she creates! She offers painting and creativity retreats, coach-

es creatives and those seeking to create greater, and she facilitates Access Consciousness®
Core Classes, internationally.

She uses her natural gifts of creating guided journeys in her creativity classes that are
specifically designed to allow the class participants to directly experience the process of creation as a flow from a space of curiosity and
play, rather than approaching it from a linear
point of view based on structure and thinking.
Painting, for her, is an experience that cannot
be 'taught'. She acknowledges the artist and
creator in everyone, and is brilliant at guiding from behind so each person can find their
gifts and choose the change they are willing to
have.

Class participants overall take with them a
greater sense of joy for their lives, inspiration
to create and ease with their being after having taken a class with Bettina.

To find Bettina's classes and see her artwork
please visit: www.BettinaStar-Rose.com and
http://BettinaMadini.Accessconsciousness.
com.

Bettina Madini's paintings are expressive, colorful and free-spirited. Painting is, for her,
more than an expression of an exterior experience, but rather a journey that reveals
itself in the process. "I love to inspire others
with my paintings and, actually, with everything I create!", she says, "I move beyond

the image that I see with my physical eyes, and allow the inner world to flow into my paintings. And how wonderful if my work inspires the viewer into more and greater and sets their own imagination free! Imagine the world that is possible if we all choose more joy and happiness each day! If I can inspire that in one person, I'm brilliantly successful!"

Bettina's paintings can be found in corporate and private collections in Europe, Australia and in the United States.

Bettina is a Certified Access Consciousness Facilitator and offers sessions and classes in the United States and abroad. Her multilingual capacities allow her to facilitate with ease and joy in English, German and French. Participants express a greater sense of who they truly are as infinite beings, expanded joy and a refreshed inspiration for creating their lives. If you would like to book a personal session with Bettina or invite her to your area for a class, contact her at bettina@bettinamadini. com. She is happy to travel near and far!

Access Consciousness® was founded by Gary Douglas. All the tools in this article are derived from Access Consciousness. Read more about Access Consciousness at www.AccessConsciousness.com.

CHAPTER 2

DO I NOT BELONG
OR AM I A UNICORN?

Cory Michelle

Why don't I belong here?

I was trapped. Trapped in a body, on a planet, in a world that valued everything I didn't. Have you ever had the thought *"Everyone is insane here?"*

I did. Often and from a very young age. Somehow I knew. I was certain I landed on the wrong planet, there must have been a mistake. Where I was from, people were kind to each other, systems were for people's best interests, meanness was not valuable, the planet was celebrated, bodies were celebrated. Screaming, empty threats, ignoring, torment, sacrifice, torture were not valued in my world.

When I was 12, I noticed that church was popular amongst my friends, going to Mass, praying, confessing their sins. I was curious and confused. Friends invited me to their church functions, and I attended a few Sunday services and each time I left confused. I couldn't wrap my head around any of it. The practice of going weekly to a place where you hear stories that sound ridiculously untrue, and you are encouraged and socialized to become a believer in all that didn't make sense, to me at least. To give up all individual thought to believe, to have faith.

Was I the only one who saw the insanity here? I wondered why people couldn't see what I saw, I wondered why people kept going back when the Pastor was declaring that everyone was a sinner for some story that happened thousands of years ago. Why was having a body wrong? What was the value of being wrong? As time went by, my friends were indoctrinated into a belief system at a young age to not think for themselves, to dismiss curiosity. You were never to think for yourself. You were inherently wrong for being alive.

"Dad, I don't believe in all this religion stuff everyone is into." I stated with confidence and a furrowed brow at age 12.

"Well, Cory, what do you believe? How did we get here?" My dad replied.

"It makes more sense to me that we were placed here by aliens and are just one big science experiment." In that moment, I became aware that I did not belong here, nor did I fit in, and I definitely wasn't trying. There was the reality everyone else was in, and then there was mine.

I feel fortunate, my parents did not enjoy church as kids and never forced it upon me, never trained me to believe in anything but myself. They allowed me to be curious and explore whatever I desired. I picked the perfect parents for me right? But even having this space and freedom, I was even more an outcast from the kids at school.

Fast forward to high school. High school was years of being different, not feeling like I fit in, never really belonging anywhere on top of being mega aware of the insanity of the way people function on Earth. I was frustrated, angry, and didn't desire to be here any longer. I had tried so hard to be cool, to fit in, to wear the right clothes, to do all the right things, but all I had done was cut off more and more of me just to be liked, and that really didn't work anyway.

In order to fit in, I developed some super powers. Well at the time, I would not have called them super powers, but burdens and I really didn't know what they were. My intuitive capacities could show me what people were thinking, and where they were functioning from. In other words, I could sniff out a liar, or someone who had it in them to cause harm. I could also feel the pain of the world and predict the future.

I remember one specific gal in high school that from the moment I met her I didn't trust her. Everyone else seemed to love her, befriended her and I was shamed for not liking her. Something was off and I knew it, so I stayed away from her. Later that year, she ended up stealing items and money from many who trusted her.

The choice not to trust her was obvious to me, but not to others. This same scenario has repeated itself a hundred times, each time me receiving judgment for others for not trusting, for being recluse and for leaving relationships when I knew betrayal was about to transpire.

From about every angle I was teased, judged, made wrong. My body being the tallest in most of my classes, for being athletic and winning awards, for being smart, for not wearing 'cool' clothes, for having big feet, for having braces for four years, for pretty much everything.

The weird thing was that most everyone liked me. But I didn't like me, so my reality occurred to me that no one really liked me. Because of that belief, I created more and more separation from people.

Senior year of high school, something strange occurred. The seniors voted on the top male and female students, with three criteria, and I won. Miss didn't fit in basically won a popularity contest. What? I didn't think much of it, I won and didn't really know what it meant for 15 years.

I obtained a scholarship to play softball at the University of Southern Colorado, and within weeks of being on the team, I saw through our coach and knew I couldn't trust her. I did have some courage and a voice I used often and had a meeting with her about it a lie she told to the team. Much to my dismay, she didn't come clean and apologize like I hoped, she mostly ostracized me for the season.

For my second year of college, I transferred to University of Colorado Boulder, quit softball (even though I had won another award for highest batting average in the region and could have had a scholarship to another school).

I made the choice to transfer based on not fitting in, and I made the choice for that school based on not feeling like I was good enough to go to a Division 1 league school.

Upon my entrance to CU, I really wanted to be accepted to the business school, but I wasn't. I never questioned how I could get in after my transfer, I just picked another major, Speech Pathology. In my final year, I was told that I should probably become an audiologist because my grades weren't good enough to be a speech pathologist. I buried the comment in my Cory's "wrong, doesn't fit in or belong here" file with the thousands of other evidence.

As I was considering what jobs I'd apply for all

I was qualified for after my university degree was a \$5.75/hour position. The thought of getting a regular job, with that little pay was devastating, scary, and I couldn't even force myself to do it.

Instead, someone had introduced me to the world of network marketing.

This was one of the first times I had been around people that were thinking and living out of the box. So I joined up and gave it a go.

About that same time I attended my first transformational seminar, where they uncovered for the first time in my life, what I had always known. We were in a matrix-like reality. What we thought was real and true, mostly wasn't. In that three days I peeled back the layers of lies I had been living from, the stories, and set me into a different direction in life. Maybe I wasn't so wrong after all?

Or was I?

The evidence continued rolling in...my Multi-Level Marketing (MLM) opportunity failed along with a few other business ventures, I was partying every weekend, working a job I hated, living with an asshole, and didn't know how to change anything. I was trapped in a world where I knew I wasn't a victim, but I sure felt like one. I started to believe that the evidence that I was obviously a failure was piling up so fast, I didn't know what I could do to change it.

Fast forward a few years. Remember that award I won in high school? One day, it hit me. **Who I thought I was and who I was being were two totally different people.** My points of view about me were not at all what others saw in me. My entire life people said I had potential, was a strong leader, was brave, had confidence, was beautiful, made a difference for them, people could count on me. But I never saw myself that way, never. I only could perceive how wrong I was, how I didn't belong and how I wasn't like anyone I knew. The judgment of myself was masking who I was naturally already being. And that award, like a flash in a moment, I could perceive how others saw me in high school.

I was living two lives and had no idea.

Since that awakening moment, I began to acknowledge who I am being, instead of believing the judgments. You know what happened? I became happier, and started enjoying me! When I released the judgments, more of the gift, brilliance and being of me could show up and life started getting better.

I started becoming even more brave about coming out of the closet with my spiritual beliefs (that happened to change daily it seemed), noticing that the more I was me in every area, the more fun I had in life. The more people enjoyed me, and the more life simply worked.

Then like a 2x4 to the back of the head, I realized I didn't come here to fit in. I will never belong to this reality. I am totally weird, different, wacky, and trying to fit in to a world where it's not ok to be you, not ok to show your unicorn horn loud and proud, is simply not for me.

I came to create new realities, to wake up, to be me, none of which can occur if I am not as much of me I can be in any moment.

Any, I mean any little tiny bit of judgment, wrongness destroys the gift that each one of us is. Everything from judging our bodies, to judging celebrities, to thinking that you've been wrong your entire life. None of that is true. None of it. Not one tiny ounce of it is true.

That was a hard one for me to swallow at first, I mean, I had always been wrong, not enough or good enough, that's what I based all my choices on.

What if every choice I made was perfect? Wait, what? No way, I had to clean up all my past choices, everywhere I had judged anyone, and confess all my mistakes! Well that is one thing I learned along the way that perpetuated the wrongness of me.

But you know where the judgment of me and all those choices got me? Exactly where I am today. Every terrible boyfriend, every interesting choice with money, every risk with business opportunities, all the credit card debt, the drugs, the extra weight, all of it. I am where I am because of EVERY choice I ever made, none of them were wrong or a mistake.

And you know what? I love, adore, appreciate and am grateful beyond words for who I be today. I am happy to have the freedom and space to create new realities, unicorn horn and all.

Releasing the judgment of me wasn't the easiest thing to do, it took being willing to see where I bought a misconception, someone else's projection, and being willing to acknowledge how psychic and aware I really am. So much of what I am aware of, that I thought was mine to deal with, to fix, to live with, was actually not. Being willing to acknowledge that everywhere I thought I had a wrongness is actually a strongness! What a relief, there is nothing wrong or broken with me, I just didn't come to do this reality, I came to create new ones. I came to be me, be joy, and break the rules of this reality. I am no longer trapped by the judgment, or this reality, it's all just really interesting, and now unicorns, what else is CRAZY POSSIBLE™?

So I do wonder, did you come to fit in, or did you too come to create new realities? The truth will set you free!

ABOUT THE AUTHOR

CORY MICHELLE

Cory Michelle, CMFW is one busy Unicorn! She's the creator of the Crazy Possible Experiment™, a renowned certified Access Consciousness® facilitator, a gifted speaker, teacher, and visionary on a mission. In addition to hosting a popular radio series and being a top-selling author, she creates and leads virtual and live programs and events for people who are ready to experience lives of ease, abundance and joy.

Some say Cory Michelle makes 'magic'... but what she actually does is teach people how to activate and harness the intuition and magic *that resides within*. She is the original Unicorn Whisperer.

Learn more about Cory Michelle at:
www.meetcorymichelle.com

CHAPTER 3

DEAR JUDGMENT

Petrina Fava

Dear Judgment... we're breaking up.

We've been together for an eternity; I know. It's been so long I was beginning to consider that there was never even a time without you; but there was. And I'd like to get back to that now.

I have glimpses of us in the beginning. I began to notice you from the corner of my eye, back when I knew I was magic and let myself spill forth into the world with exuberance. I was being all of me, exploring the world in awe and shining so brightly just for fun. Just for me.

Silently, you crept into my world. You were smooth and slick. Disguised in pretty colours, you had people telling me I was smart, beautiful, talented, and special. It was fantastic. Slowly and ever so quietly, you took from my hands all I knew of my own brilliance and placed it on the outside; into the validation of others until I could no longer find it within myself. Soon, you morphed into physical form.

Gold stars, report cards, trophies, ribbons, awards; seemingly bright and shiny objects that were meager representations of my immeasurable gifts. They distracted me as you stole my magic. The self-assured certainty of my own brilliance was snuffed out by your presence; my knowing meant nothing compared to the objects and words of validation from others.

I began to hear your voice as my own, hammering down the mallet of discrimination between right and wrong; good and bad. Hungrily and swiftly, you began to turn our dance in different directions and our pace quickened at an amazing speed, spiralling at every turn. We gathered the world up into our dance and I felt you all around me; tasted the depths of you. Before long, we were so intertwined that I couldn't sense where you ended and I began. I noticed you in others, but you assured me that you were only mine and I felt your presence strongly.

You pointed out my mis-steps, my errors. You showed them to me zealously under the guise of caring and I understood that this would set me straight where I was getting it all wrong. I had only desired to joyfully dance my way through life, but you showed me the error of my ways. You became louder, more commanding. I used you to motivate me into being better, to correct myself, to make myself right in all the many places I was wrong. You demanded I remove my head from the clouds, place my steps carefully and keep a little fear in my back pocket to ensure we didn't ever fall. You revealed where I was mistaken about magic, mistaken about trust, mistaken about my brilliance and the beauty of others. "Do not be blinded by beauty," you warned. "Take off your rose-coloured glasses, the world is a frightful place". All I had ever thought to be my brilliance was actually my weakness, you told me; everything I considered wonderful about me was actually my greatest downfall. You revealed where others felt smaller when I was shining too brightly and you told me how unkind I was being. You explained that I was vain in thinking I was brilliant. You glorified humility and molded me into a feeble martyr. You unveiled all those who disapproved of my brilliance. All of this weighed heavily on me and the approval of others became an intense need. I reached for it constantly to fill the empty space that once held my knowing. Somehow, approval felt comfortable even though it was enormously painful to shrink myself smaller. I wanted more validation. You told me what I needed to do. It hurt, but I cut off my wings, extinguished my magic and retracted my bright rays of sunshine. I bent and coiled myself to fit the expectations of others. Then suddenly I was tripping and falling at every turn. I spiraled further and further into the wrongness of me with such velocity that I barely recognized the dance anymore. I tried to twist myself into the right steps but could never seem to escape the tornado of errors. Occasionally, there was a brief and distant memory of magic, wings and sunshine. I vowed to forget these and convinced myself they were lies. As we performed on a larger stage with each passing year, my brilliance was all but gone and the wrongness of me was an ever growing block of heavy cement encompassing my feet.

Finally, we are here and I can no longer move. Our dance has come to a screeching halt. I'm looking to you, judgment, but you're no longer helping me and nothing is changing. I cry out "Please! I don't know any other way except you!" but you only sneer and watch me struggle, tightening your grip harder than ever. Staring down at the cement blocks and knowing only you, I feel trapped. I am confused as you stand and laugh wickedly while I reach for you, the only tool for change I have ever known. What am I to do now? What else is there besides you, judgment? You've destroyed me and I am shaking with anger and resentment at you! No matter how enraged I become and how hard I strike at the cement that encircles me I cannot release you! Vulnerable in the wake of the sudden halting of our dance, I feel the vibrating wiggle of my brilliance. I've ignored it, devalued it and hammered it down deeply. I've smothered it with you, the dark cape of unconsciousness. And yet here's my magic, its potency increased; never in fact destroyed! My beautiful wings remain; their span even greater than before. The rays of sunshine are reaching farther and bursting brighter than ever. I know they cannot extend to their farthest reach while you're here, Judgment. Please go... I beg you...

What has your insidious dance with judgment been like? Bring your awareness to a time, perhaps when you were a child, when you were being all of you. Can you perceive it? Can you recall a time when you were everything; exuberant and joyful, sad and angry, curious and in wonder of it all? Remember when you were expressing yourself freely without concern that others were observing you through their lenses of discernment? You were dancing, laughing, playing, crying, screaming; all of it at its fullest expression without any conclusion about whether it was right or wrong. You knew things without thought and perceived the world on many different levels. You could be anything and everything; you received easily from all that surrounded you. Imagine for a moment that time is not real. Do you have access to that totality of you now? You do, because your magic cannot be destroyed.

When did you decide that the approval of others was more valuable than having all of you? How much of yourself did you cut off in an effort to obtain it at all costs? When did you decide that being validated was more important than knowing your brilliance? Have you become so aware of other people's judgments that you hear them in your own head? How loud are their unspoken judgments to your awareness and how long have you been buying them as your own? Would you be willing to see that they are not yours?

Judgment has become the unquestioned fabric of this reality. It is so ingrained in our world that most of us don't even notice it for what it is anymore. It is valued as the road to improvement, but how much do you have to make yourself wrong in order to be right? How much energy does it take to judge yourself out of your wrongness and what is this doing to your body? Judgment will never take you out of wrongness and into greatness.

Judgment can only create more judgment; each one requires many others to hold it in place. A tangled, heavy block of lies engulfs you until you can no longer see your true beauty and the unique gift you are to the world. Judgment may place its dark, heavy cloak over your brilliance. You yourself may do your very best to cut off the most beautiful parts and pieces of you; the ones that shine too brightly for others to see. This is an illusion; it may be temporarily dimmed, but your brilliance remains. Judgments are lies; all of them. Judgment is not real. There is an easier way to change something that is not working for you. It is possible to create greater without judging yourself as less than you are now.

I look at the cement that encompasses my feet, sigh deeply and close my eyes. I see now. I chose you, Judgment. I invited you into my world and used you because you were all I knew. I lower my walls of resistance to you. You have no power and I am no victim. Our dance has contributed to my life and brought me to this moment. I have a new awareness of what is true for me now, and for this I am deeply grateful. I am lighter suddenly and as I open my eyes the cement is gone. Goodbye judgment. You've served me well, but we're breaking up. I choose ME.

About the Author

PETRINA FAVA

An International #1 Best-selling Author of "Creations: Conscious Fertility and Conception, Pregnancy and Birth" and "Possibilities in Parenting," Petrina is also the host of her own radio show "Messy Adventures in Living" on a2zen.fm. You can find Petrina exploring her capacities and discovering more of her magic every day, but it hasn't always been this way. At the age of 12, Petrina Fava placed a book order at school. On the day that they arrived, while all the kids were comparing their books, Petrina realized she was getting strange looks from the others. While everyone else had chosen storybooks, Petrina had purchased one called "How to Get Straight A's". There was snickering. This was the moment Petrina realized that her desire to create something greater for herself was not considered cool amongst her peers. She was weird. She continued to be drawn to "self-help" books and read many of them eagerly, but she certainly didn't tell anyone about it. She wanted to be liked. So she kept most of her real curiosities secret, and tried her best to be interested in normal things like television shows, nail polish colors and makeup. She spent most of her high school years judging herself harshly for not being like everyone else and trying hard to fit in. It didn't work, thank goodness.

Petrina continued to be intrigued by "new age" books about dreams, psychic abilities and life after death. Throughout high school, she was in awe as she learned about the many intricate systems of the body and was amazed at its ability to heal and change, create life out of two tiny little cells and manage detailed and highly complex functions; all seemingly with its own intelligence. She knew without a doubt that she wanted to work with bodies. She also knew that she was kind and caring, and chose to study Nursing in University. Petrina continues to work with children and their families at SickKids in Toronto. She learned to teach Infant Massage and started her own business, Gentle Connections, in 2008.

Still, after years of studying well documented medical and nursing knowledge about bodies, Petrina's interest in the "weird" stuff continued. She knew there was something else, something more. At the age of 35, she became a Reiki Practitioner and was excited to play with energy. It felt like magic. She discovered the tools of Access Consciousness in 2009 and has been playing with its tools and creating her life in all kinds of unexpected ways since then. In addition to teaching Infant Massage, she is teaching Kids Yoga, *GROOVE* Dance and has created her own line of natural skin care products called *Naturally Happy Body.* Petrina is an Access Bars and Body Process Facilitator as well as a Right Body for You Intro Facilitator. The Access tools have empowered Petrina to increase her awareness, acknowledge her capacities, drop the self-judgment and step into her potency to create greater. She is excited to empower others to create their own lives by offering Access Consciousness BARS and Body Process sessions, Access Consciousness classes, as well as writing and participating in speaking engagements. As a mom of three, Petrina uses the empowering tools of Access Consciousness to create ease with parenting. Her amazing children continue to show her all the places she is holding onto judgment and fear, and they provide plenty of opportunities to let all of that go and replace it with laughter. She has discovered that all along the magic has been right in her own hands.

You are invited to connect with Petrina at any of the following:

www.petrinafava.com
www.facebook.com/petrinafavachoosinghappy
www.petrina.fava.accessconsciousness.com
http://a2zen.fm/podcast/messy-adventures-
in-living-petrina-fava/

CHAPTER 4

HOW MUCH FUN ARE YOU WILLING TO HAVE WITH JUDGMENT?

Pia Jansson

The energy of judgment is an interesting one to me, it's easy for me to look at my own judgments, as I'm aware of what they are at this point and then there's receiving judgment from others. To me, I've found that it all depends on who it comes from and how it is delivered. I rarely get triggered nowadays, and when I do it will spur an action in me. For one, I always tend to self reflect and look at what part I took in creating this, and then I look at what the other person's intention was. I've realized that what triggers me is when it's someone really close to me is not accepting or hearing what I have to say and starts to question my point of view while I'm being vulnerable, tired or simply not prepared to have a discussion.

I have someone in my life right now that has a communication style that is very different from mine, most of the time we get along great, and at times the delivery and projected points of views are misinterpreted and down the rabbit hole we go. What I appreciate about this person is that we ride the energy out until we've cleared it, speak frankly about what we were intending to communicate, and take responsibility for our actions and behaviors. The funny thing is that while all this is happening I know that we are caught in an energy that is not even ours to begin with and we often have very similar points of view, we simply express it in different ways!

The more I have started to acknowledge my awareness, the more I realize how much more I pick up from my surroundings that often is not even my points of view. I tend to catch myself when I find myself speaking about something that is not really my point of view, often with laughter. And then at other times it takes creating a situation where I totally lose myself, where I get deflated, contracted and realize how I have totally stopped being me and I just look for a way to flee. Where all the tools I have access to have evaporated from my awareness AND then there's the moment when I catch myself. I find myself immediately taking a few deep breaths, moving my body to shake the energy off and then I start asking questions like "Who does this belong to®?", "Who am I being right now?", "What's right about this that I am not getting?", "Interesting point of view he/she has that point of view" and all the Access Consciousness® clearings that I can think of. And before I know it, I have my space and joy back again.

I may judge myself that I even got hooked and later on I realize that I was being what was required in that moment. That being vulnerable and open is powerful, especially when two or more people are truly committed to communicating with and understanding each other fully and it doesn't always show up in a desired way of being from your point of view. And the realization that in the scope of things not very much time was actually spent in drama mode. What happens with me with one person in particular is an immense sense and depth of gratitude for staying with me through conversations where we have different perspectives until we sort it out, in the end empowering both parties. Ultimately we are building an intimacy and trust with each other that is beyond what we have been willing to commit to prior to this and that makes it exciting to me.

Then there are other situations with other people not as close, or strangers, and there I find it a little bit more ease-filled. For example, when someone cuts you off in traffic, do you get upset? Years ago when I lived in Chicago I used to listen to the rock stations. With traffic being intense and people driving very close to your bumper on the highway I would find myself getting hooked into the stress and aggression around me. And then one day I flipped the channels and ended up on a laid-back coastal station and in a second shifted my mood into an easy-going happy and relaxed one. I started laughing to myself and got the power of how easily we can shift how we feel and react by simply choosing music that supports what we desire to create, and from that moment on listened to relaxing music while driving.

In my life, I've found that sweating the small stuff is not worth it, and making small changes can create big changes. Zipping my mouth and allowing people to speak and complete their thoughts takes practice and patience yet it's all worth it when you see what it often creates. Being on the receiving end of being able to share your thoughts, feelings and opinions without being interrupted or judged is an immense gift. As I started having more friends and acquaintances in my circles that could listen to me without a point of view I was able to release so many opinions that I had carried within me that I wasn't even aware of, how cool is that? And there is no bigger gift than to be heard, seen and listened to without judgment, from my point of view. I've found that when you speak with someone who can allow you to be without a point of view it not only heals your past, it creates an immense gratitude and trust for the person willing to hold that space for you.

I've often held space for others throughout my life; it comes easy for me and is something that I didn't think much of. I knew that people often trusted me quickly and felt safe to be around me. It wasn't until I started receiving the same with people other than my close friends that I really got the immense value of it. And how often do people actually acknowledge that value? I guess it all depends on your reality and point of view.

I've listened and spoken to many people over the years who were judged for being and expressing their authentic selves. The pain they carried for all the judgments they had received created a lot of pain and suffering. My point of view or motto has always been "be yourself" as I and many of us get that intuitive hit that something is "off" when we are not. Sure being you takes courage, especially when you are expressing yourself in a different way than your surroundings, whether it shows on the outside or not. The power of being you though makes it a lot easier to live and create your life from my point of view even when people throw judgments on you.

And while it's easy to give up who you are in the face of judgment standing up for yourself by simply being, without defending who you are, or who you are not, being you creates simplicity and self-confidence long-term as you ultimately are honoring you. When I look back at how many of our inspirational world leaders created their lives and wealth they did it by not caving into other people's points of view, staying true to themselves, speaking up without necessarily being confrontational. That's the fine line after all. Being able to speak to what people can receive and hear.

Many paid a price, like Martin Luther King, yet look at what got created afterwards. And then there's Sir Richard Branson who created his life and businesses on his terms, with PR stunts that received loads of judgment yet look at where he is now? And Oprah, the contribution that she has been to this planet is extra-ordinary, all while being herself.

We all start from nothing, some with a clear vision from the get-go, others following an inner guidance energy, and some of us simply try a bunch of stuff until we find what we are looking for. To me I know that the key is tapping into that space of infinite possibilities which happens when I'm in a space of gratitude and when others are with me sharing both gratitude and a willingness to be in the space of no judgment.

And at times it's the judgment of others or myself that has me spring into action. Either way, there are tons of tools available and the key is to find the tools that ultimately empower and work for you and putting them all into practice. As with anything in life creating some sort of practice or action is what makes the difference in addition to simply being your true authentic self. It could be asking questions and clearing any energy that stops you from an awareness or action, it could be creating a vision board, prayer, meeting up with people that empower you, and mastermind or create accountability partners that are a stand for you.

The most important part is to simply choose to take that first step, be a demand to believe in you, independent on what other people think of you, and to include you in the equation even when you have a giving nature. Depleting yourself doesn't create. Remember, even the stewards of the airplane announces to put on your oxygen mask first before your child. It is OK to be selfish! Let's face it, if you don't care for you, who will? Is your happiness not up to you to generate? And what can get created when two or more people come together that know that?

To me that is the beginning steps of creating any type of friendship. Being with people that are being and honoring themselves and their needs are very attractive qualities to me. Add to that humor, laugher, playfulness, spontaneity and fun and I'm a happy camper and when I'm happy guess what? Other people tend to feel better too.

When I tap into the space of infinite possibilities and spring into action and share my creative expressions I also inspire others to do the same for them. All from surrounding myself with people that have a powerful listening of no judgment! It's priceless and can't be bought. It generates and expands continuously and I'll have that any day.

Judgment on the other hand kills possibility on so many levels. I think many times we do not necessarily intend to judge, and this includes "good and bad" judgments, much of it is simply behaviors that we have taken on, learned from others and until we stop long enough and really look at what the energy creates whether projected towards ourselves or from someone else it's easy to keep going. So while we all have days or moments when we go through a spectrum of awareness, judgments, moods, etc., it's ultimately a choice and commitment to stay present every moment of the day.

Distractions are so easy to get hooked into when we are not ready to "be" or deal with something, and nowadays with social media and cell phones it's easier than ever to disconnect from the realities that we have created. And then something happens and we stop maybe long enough to actually commit to something different, one step at the time and with time something new is created.

I used to be friendly and smile at everyone I met, strangers as well as friends, over the years I started picking up that it wasn't being received (=judgment) and eventually I stopped smiling as frequently to strangers. It became more important to fit in and not stir the water than to display one feature of me that comes easy. After allowing this for a while I lost myself, who I was and what my contribution to this planet was/is. All from no longer saying hello and smiling. I started looking at that in more depth and realized that some of that came from a determination of not allowing unhappy people zap my mojo, yet it was also a game that created so much fun for me. It energized me, was an easy action to take and I was befriended by people all the time.

I'm still recovering from being with the judgment of what a smile or laughter is for some people and I'm still in the process of taking the power back and to be more of me no matter how people around me responds. After all if I'm not being me what's the point?

So what did you give up on in your life? What desires did you put aside to focus on something else? Is now the time to take even five minutes of your time each day to do something that empowers you? Listening to a song that creates joy, taking a walk, meeting up or talking with a friend, creating something with your hands? Whatever sparks joy in you is for you.

I've explored many personal and business modalities over the years and in Access Consciousness® I have found a set of tools and processes that expands my awareness with ease, while having loads of fun and laughter present. Many of the questions in this chapter originated from there. The game is to ask questions without answering them and to tap into the awareness you have in what's true for you. Would you like to play? More information can be found at www.AccessConsciousness. com. And if you so desire, here are some questions I use that come from Access Consciousness that could maybe be fun to play with to see what you desire to create in your life that would be expansive for you: "If I choose this what will my life look like in five years? If I don't choose it what will my life look like in five years?"

One of the options will pull on you, whether by an inner joy type of feeling, lightness or expansiveness in your body = yes and the other option will have more of sinking feeling = no. The key here to note is that what is a yes for you could be a no for someone else, so trust your gut instincts and play with the questions, before you know it a new path has been created that is true to you and what you desire to create. And what I've found is that when I ask these questions it also takes into consideration the values and beliefs that are important to me.

The more I take the actions that are true to me, that empower me, no judgment in the world can stop me. I also have more capacity to be with people that choose to judge, and can allow them to be whomever they choose to be without it affecting my well-being. So I wonder, what would this planet be like if people chose to be happy and grateful? What would it be like to travel, live and create on a planet where people where being themselves and creating a life that empowered them? Does that sound like fun to you? What action can you take for you to empower and inspire you right now? How much fun are you willing to receive? Is there such a thing as having too much fun?

About the Author

PIA JANSSON

 As far back as I can remember I have been coaching people, and I started my coaching business in 2005. I love being part of the process of facilitating change in people's lives and businesses. Continual growth and exploration of who I am, shedding values and beliefs that no longer serve me to free up the space to be me, all of me, all the time, is a moment by moment choice that I prioritize. I thrive on change and learning new things every day, being playful, silly, having FUN, and laughing daily. I am fascinated about space on all levels, having expansive conversations in any area of life and to live and go beyond the "box" of whatever "normal" is. I am an Access Consciousness® Bars Facilitator and Access Consciousness® Body Process Facilitator, and an ordained Minister through the Universal Life Church Monastery.

I've spent many years in the corporate world, building and reorganizing business areas and I also started up a subsidiary from scratch, as one of the co-creators instrumental to creating the foundation that exists today. My philosophy in general is that what I don't know I'll figure out.

If you would like to read my blog or book a session with me go to www.space-2-play.com. With joy and gratitude,

CHAPTER 5

THE JOY OF CHANGING FIXED POSITIONS

Rebecca Hulse

Judgment is an energy that can hound our whole lives, ruining it and leaving the possibilities of a future in a desiccated mess. However, it's something that can also be completely irrelevant, a gift even... if we let it.

One of my favorite ways to explore a topic is to look into the energy of the word. Most words in the English language have misidentified definitions, as the dictionaries have been changed many times to suit politics and colloquial use. However most dictionaries pre-1946 have unaltered and more true acknowledgements of the word's energetic meaning.

The word 'release' is defined as *deliverance, liberation, from trouble, sorrow, life, duty, confinement or fixed position.* What strikes me the most out of these energies is the one: *liberation from a fixed position.*

This is exactly what judgment is – taking on a

fixed point of view and functioning from it. The limitation isn't from the point of view; having a point of view can make your life interesting and entertaining. What matters is how fluid and changeable it is, the looser your grip on the point of view, the easier your life can be.

However if you're functioning and living *through* your points of view, they solidify into a judgment and start to inhibit your ability to choose, change and see possibilities. I found this quote recently and it struck me profoundly on a few different levels with the simultaneous simplicity and depth:

> *"By being natural and sincere, one often can create revolutions without having sought them."*
> — Christian Dior

What I see in this is when you are willing to be you, without affectation, trying to be anything else, or acting for anything, just by your very being waltzing through life, you create change. Doesn't this seem to melt away the desire for judgment of any kind?

Truly, I have seen time and time again in myself and countless others, the best moments of their enjoyment of life, creations, wondrous inexplicable moments and dreams, all stem forth from the point where they chose to let go everything that isn't them.

The secret I found out though, is that it's not

one big choice that will suddenly snowball into all these phenomenal events coming to fruition. It's small, daily, persistent, never-ending choices.

It's not one choice that will set you free but the willingness to choose and choose again until looking, choosing and changing becomes the way of functioning.

Our way of being is actually more fluid and changeable than we think. Do we often hear we need to "Develop our personality" or "Stick to your guns" or "How much energy does that take?" (Truly, how much fun is it truly to be the same all the time?)

However if you're willing to be different in every 10 seconds, you can live every day as a new adventure and never have the same day twice in a row. That's not because the day is different, but because you are choosing different.

Imagine if you looked back one year and you could never identify a boring day or a day that was average, the same or like any other. What if every day and every moment could be remarkable?

There is no massive secret wisdom to be revealed about releasing judgment. There are tools that can assist, however if I spend hours and hours on the subject of choice and a few minutes writing about some tools I know, that can also assist my hope that you will go for the different possibility this time and try out-choosing.

It's commonly idealized to go for magic wands, elixirs, tools, processing, clearing and eliminating limitations, however no matter the tool or the efficacy, these can only erase your past and everything you created that creates your life as it currently is.

It cannot create your future. The only tool I have found that can assist you in creating a future is choosing.

Gary Douglas, the Founder of Access Consciousness® says:

> "Until you commit to your life you are in a constant state of judgment of you. Once you commit, the judgment subsides."

My question to you is, are you choosing your life?

The moment you actually choose to create something, it creates a ripple effect in the Universe, to create this "new life" as a reality. When you chose to not be at the effect of this reality, succumbing to judgments and limitations don't have to be a part of your world. If you don't create your reality, this reality will do it for you – it paints with a lot more limited possibilities than you have access to.

Release does not have to be some long stren-
uous event to shake off the judgment, it can
also be the action of liberating yourself from
your chosen confinement. Without previous
definition to go by, would this now not seem
simple and easier than you imagined?

If you could choose a life of creating every day,
would you include judgment in your world? Or
would it become something like the trash of
your reality? Nothing to really remark or dwell
upon, just something to dispose of.

What if judgment was less of an extremely significant attack, and instead just an invitation
to acknowledge for a second and move on? The
main challenge you may choose isn't to release
judgment but the resistance to changing your
point of view than anything else.

What have you decided is so great about having judgment in your universe anyway?

Did you finally get it right?

If you judge you first, then no one else can
judge you as harshly?

Are you judging yourself 'positively' as if that's
better?

The only point of view that doesn't limit the
possibilities of your life is one you're willing
to change. There is no wrongness in having a
point of view (if you're going to have one, it may

as well be interesting and fascinating to you!), the test is if you're willing to lose it, change it or if you have a strange contractive almost 'needy' desire to keep it.

When these strange thoughts pop into your head, or you have a strong view towards something, ask yourself "Would I be willing to change this? Or am I holding on with dear life to this judgment?"

Change doesn't have to be a struggle; it can actually be a fun adventure – especially if you're willing to have a bit of fun with yourself along the way. The judgment you may become aware of, that you're currently possessing, may be harsher or more rigid than you think – lightness and humor will change this faster than any force or struggle you may do.

Then once you incorporate other people's judgments and points of view of themselves, you and everything in between the game becomes event greater! A great mentor of mine said: *"Strength comes from the willingness to be that which other people judge as wrong."* He has a great joy in stirring up people's points of views and then having such a joy and lightness with it – in this choice, all the points of view start to dissolve.

What gift can you be for yourself and others by your willingness to be the lightness that any solid point of view dissolves into fun and entertainment?

Please note: Not everyone will take kindly and enjoy your natural dissolve of their point of view, they fought very hard and long to keep it, and rightfully so! Some people really do enjoy judgment so please don't do them the disservice of removing it.

However, what you chose, create and be for you in your own life is completely up to you, luckily! There is no boss over-lording you picking the correct points of view out of your head and removing the unruly ones. You get to be the wonderful master of your own life.

A wonderful living inspiration of mine, Chutisa Bowman, had a phenomenal conversation that I use every time I'm unwilling to lead and be for myself what would create a phenomenal life. This is my best rendition and artistic expansion in my own imagination:

> *If you were the CEO of your own life, what would you choose?*
>
> *Would you keep all the people? Or would you fire some? How about what you're creating today and for the future? Does it excite you as CEO or would you say "Next idea!"? Do you like the working conditions or are there a few upgrades and repairs in order?*

Notice none of this conversation is about judging you or your life, simply asking you to be aware of what is and what you desire. This is the power of releasing judgment; you get to have your awareness of what is truly going on for you and whether it works.

Have you ever had a day where you feel like you're walking around blind? Surprise after not-so-delightful surprise throws itself at you and you don't know what to think. All you can sense is that as the day goes by you are slowly feeling more contracted, and life is dull.

This is the life led by judgment; you no longer get to receive this wonderful indefinable gift called awareness, where you simply know in the flash of a second what choosing something would create for you. Awareness isn't about cognitive psychic reading where you can get a clear worded or visual definition of something like a thought.

Awareness works in all mediums and it's up to you to receive it and it doesn't have to be cognitive.

So how in the world do you do that? You can't think about it, you don't know what it looks like and you have no idea what it really means either. Have you ever had something inexplicable happen in your life or maybe many? You didn't think about it, you don't know what it looked like and you have no idea what it really means either?

There's a common misconception that if it's

not explainable, conceivable or definable it's impossible. However nature shows us every day that it doesn't require any of those prerequisites to do what it desires to do ever!

So who are we to limit, define and restrict ourselves? What if it wasn't natural?

It takes a considerable amount of energy to stop yourself from being what is natural to you. Have you ever tried to write with your other hand or pretend to be someone for a day? How long did it take before it was exhausting? What if having awareness was the same?

If you let it in, no matter how bizarre and strange and inconceivable, what comes to you is you start to develop a reality without limits and without judgment. You only have to ask for it. And ask of yourself that you demand it.

What is it you have been denying you have a desire to ask for? The crazy thing is you might actually receive it (and enjoy it!). What we tend to do is make up an entire story in our heads about what makes this something you can't have or a bad thing that you have long since forgotten. How many decisions have you made against what you desire to create the judgments that limit your world?

Did that sentence make your brain jump? It's designed to access the energy of what you have decided, in the illogical part of your mind that stores these forgotten decisions and judgments that create your life as it is.

Is it time to let those go?

What will your life be like if you continue maintaining your current point of view for the rest of your life? Or only change a few? Does this trajectory match the life you dream of creating? Or does it sorely disappoint?

Your point of view creates your reality. And as I mentioned before, you get to choose those points of view or to even have them at all. What interesting point of view could you create that would allow the judgments to fall away, the decisions that hold in place your limits dissolve, and allow you to start painting the canvas of your life with the elements you choose?

You are a fortunate infinite being born with a capacity to create, and to create anything you can with the barest hints to start with. It could be asking a question, a vague awareness of an energy, or the inkling of a possibility.

What if releasing judgment was not about finding what was wrong with you and trying to reason yourself out of holding onto it but gracefully choosing to create, and enjoy the possibilities all around you with no point of view? Changing it any 10 seconds you like?

Welcome to your world.

About the Author

REBECCA HULSE

 *Rebecca Hulse is a go-getting, risk-taking millennial. She is a writer, bestselling author, the Manager/Leader of Joy of Business, Access Consciousness Certified Facilitator and creator of magnitude.*

Rebecca loves creating – business, her life, possibilities, it doesn't matter what it is as long as it's greater than what she has created before. She sees a different reality and possibility – usually far beyond this reality which she has used to create her own life traveling the world from New Zealand to Costa Rica, USA, South Africa, Australia, the Caribbean, Europe and beyond.

She is the author of four books including two Amazon #1 Best-Sellers *The Energy of Receiving* and *The Energy of Creativity,* and speaks to a global audience on consciousness, business and being. From her cozy Christchurch home in New Zealand, Rebecca Hulse reaches and traipses around a global audience. Rebecca is interested in facilitating infinite possibilities, choice and creation of magnitude including the maximization of profits, teamwork, leadership and Benevolent Capitalism.

Her writing has been featured in MindBodyGreen, NotSalmon, Wild Sister, My Yoga Online, Elephant Journal, Girlfriendology, Classy Career Girl, TeraWarner.com, OM Times, and-AccessConsiousness.com just to name a few. Rebecca Hulse is an Access Consciousness facilitator and loves taking these phenomenal Access Consciousness tools global.

You can explore possibilities with Rebecca casually on Facebook, in a private session any time via Skype or in person wherever she is, through her online programs, classes and recordings available at rebeccahulse.com and in her classes around the world.

CHAPTER 6

RELEASING JUDGMENT: POSSIBILITIES FOR CREATION BEYOND WHAT IS

Beth Schliebe

The power of releasing judgment can be explored in every aspect of life. It is an energy that affects every thought, feeling, emotion, and action of the body that can lead to creation or destruction. The energy coming from the power of releasing judgment can lead to the creation of health and healing in our bodies; however, it also can possibly lead to destruction if the choice is made to hold on to judgment. How does that happen? Let's explore.

Let's start with questions...

What would it be like if you are aware you hold the power for what you create in your own hands? What would you choose to hold on to and what would you choose to release? What if releasing judgment gave you the power to open possibilities in becoming youthful, more vibrant, happier, calmer, creative, healthier, and anything else you could choose?

Have you ever explored the concept of psychoneuroimmunology? This is a physical actualization where we experience the creation in our body of the age-old concept that "energy follows thought." This is a term that offers explanation about how our thoughts channel through our nervous system and affect our health and healing or disease and destruction. In each moment, we have a massive number of thoughts going through our minds, like a computer. The programs or thoughts often have become like a broken record, a repeat pattern, a mimicry pattern, or a virus that continually pop up in one's thinking, like in a computer.

Have you ever wondered what you are creating that is affecting your body? When did you check out and become unaware that you are the creative capacities and the choices that are resulting in your body as you know it now? If someone gave you a simple, effective formulation for changing what you didn't like about the health of your body would you even try it? Have you turned the choices for your health over to other people, cutting off what you innately know as your truth about yourself? Have you become a victim, or are you willing to be a part of your own equation and stop assuming everybody else is responsible for your outcome?

Let's talk about awareness...

We are not victims, even if sometimes it might feel that way. (What if "victim" was a judgment?). We are created with this amazing gift of being energy, space, and consciousness! What if every creation designed in our body or in our experiences is a result of "energy following our thoughts"? Then the action or words increases the intensity of the vibration channeled through the nervous system, continued to actualize in our bodies as well as in other people, places and things that we are relationship to. This is intensified energy going through our system, in and out of the body.

The body is an amazing entity! It has infinite wisdom, resources, desires, and is designed to give us information far beyond what our repeat, mimicked patterned programs have stored in the computer bank that sits on top of our shoulders. What if we really tapped into the possibility of the concept that in any moment by changing our thoughts we can change our outcome? It has often been stated in many ways, "Change the way you look at something and the thing you look at will change". Also, "Everything is the opposite of what it appears to be, nothing is the opposite of what it appears to be". These are not new concepts! Yet, they may be ones that people have not been aware of or explored. These concepts have the power to be applied to anything. YES, I mean anything!!!

Let's play some...

Take a look at the clouds, what do you see? Now ask your body what else is possible to see, if you tilt or turn your head in a different position, or try to squint your eyes. Now try to turn around, take another look, or ask someone else what they see? After looking at the same cloud from different positions, do you see different things or always the same thing? Any time we fixate on only one position in our thinking or perception, that point of view is solidified. We have lost our power of creating possibilities and gone into judgment of only one thought. Then, we make it a rule with a judgment of right or wrong to validate our position. Next we channel that through our nervous system and store that thought as a reference point that has no flexibility or fluid possibilities. It is fixed. Too many fixed judgments or points of view start creating a limited world and a finite, inflexible reality. Your body then follows the solidification and the biochemistry behind it to adjust. It flows to your posture, your structure, your tissues, your organs, your cells, your function, and all the molecules. Then all your energy is spent trying to hold together the parts breaking down, instead of creating the energy for a happy, healthy body and life.

What if you have innate creative power by releasing the judgment of how you saw the clouds, another person, your job, your home, your money, your animals, the news, the planet or especially your body? Would you be willing to play with fluidity in your point of view vs. rigidity in your thoughts and drop all those judgments? If you would, your body could release the judgments that it has been the storage dump for. Most people's storage dump is made up of the body being the container, and the brain being the computer. As our thoughts or points of view get stuck, the brain or computer runs limited programs and the body suffers systems of boredom, insanity, depression, sickness, and disease (limited function). Are you in a state of breakdown created from being a storage dump of limited points of view and judgments? What power could you reboot just by choosing to play with expanding your points of views, entertaining new thoughts or ways of doing things and dropping judgments. Just by choosing that, a different outcome is available for your health, insanity, depression, anger, blame, guilt, shame, fear, doubt, and addictions. These symptoms are actualized to try to keep control by seeing and doing things exactly the same. Does any of that sound exciting for the body to create health and healing?

Let's explore another concept...

What if everything is a relationship? So, if everything is energy and energy follows our thoughts, then whatever you are thinking about, you are in relationship with it. Also whatever you think about the most or focus on, you are expanding the energy of that relationship of it to you and you to it! Again, who is choosing what is created in your world, in your body, in your family, in your money, in your animals, in your home, in your health, and on this planet? What if just by being alive you realize that you are a creator, a generator, and a contribution? What creation or destruction are you in relationship with at this present moment? Most often we are taught we are powerless so we often choose to receive self-inflicted judgment, projected judgment and/or expected judgment.

Now look at your body, what are you obsessing over or focused on for more than 30 seconds? Now, focus on that cloud you observed before. Are you still obsessing over your body in that same moment? Now look back at your body, where you were obsessing, has it already changed or do you have to bring back the old thoughts and patterns to recreate it? What if you realized you can change the outcome of anything by releasing any stuck judgment or point of view that you have made a rule set on, so you can be right and not have to change. No one usually tells you it can be that simple. The thought that there is a problem about what you are focused on creates a problem! That's a judgment! So, do you choose judgment as your primary relationship, especially when it is about your body and the decreasing power that judgment eventually produces? Therefore, are you choosing to create the lack of power for creating the body and a healthy body in lieu of a creation of destroying the body?

If there is a problem, a statement or judgment

limits the choice of creating something different or creating differently. Often people create
a problem just to judge themselves valuable if
they can fix it and go beyond it. This often is
done unconsciously (I call it being on automatic). Then we are confused, fooled by ourselves when we wake up and wonder when
and how we got into that predicament. Next
you wonder what you were saying or thinking
that the energy was following when you were
on automatic. Can you feel your body and your
mind being jerked around or contracted by
reading all this?

What if you check in with your body, to experience the awareness of what the massive con-
tractions and heaviness or the disgust that
you are creating by those judgmental thoughts.
Where do you feel it in your body? Is it heavy?
What if you find it in your body, then tell your
body you are sorry for all the thoughts and
judgments you have been sticking it with and
ask if there is another choice? Tell your body
you will release the judgments so power for
creating something other than destruction can
occur. Does your body feel more space now or
lighter? Even the slightest bit of change has
started a shift in a different direction! What if
you acknowledge that power you have in any
moment by choosing to release the judgment
and know that your body loves non-judgment
too? What if the power for changing your body
and its health lies in choosing to release judgment? Would you be willing to explore and
play with all that?

Let's play again...

Just by awareness and acknowledgement of all that "disgust" you can choose to say "STOP" To get off the merry-go-round of judgmental insanity! Would you choose it? It only takes a moment to make a choice! In today's teaching to children there is a slogan that says, "Say no to drugs". What if judgment was the most addictive drug with the greatest internal and external detrimental effects, would you please say "no to that drug now"? Again, it only takes a moment to make a choice that can affect your whole life!

So, let's explore further! Our bodies have an innate intelligence and awareness, happy thoughts, joy, laughter, fun, and energies of that vibration actually begin to heal cell structures. The body knows what creative energies it enjoys and responds to creating health as your reward for choosing those energies. The body loves to be honored in those vibrations! Likewise, the cells change shape and form from round and healthy to elliptical and clumped when continual bombardment of negativity and judgment is the constant vibratory menu. The round happy cells shrink from the negativity in a defense, and after long enough they then began to try to hold the viral thoughts at bay. Yet those cells actually become the virus in the body, and the body then creates toxicity. It is not only toxic to the host (your body) the energy of toxicity expands outward to other people, places, and things around the earth. It actually becomes a field of energy that is carried to other people of similar thought and diseased states; that seems to lump together a bigger field (similar to the way cells lump in the body). JUDGMENT seems to have the highest toxicity scale! Judgment turned inward upon ourselves or outward toward other people, places and things can be a powerfully destructive force for all living conscious energy! So, anytime you judge yourself, an animal, another person, or anything; you not only have chosen to be a destructive energy outwardly, you have also started the process inwardly to a diseased state.

So here we are at a crossroad called awareness. One direction offers power through, choice, healing, possibility, joyful creation with fluidity, and releasing judgment. The other direction offers power through judgment, disease, addiction for control and rigidity of mind and body. Either direction is just a choice. Either direction has power, one towards creation and one towards destruction. What choice would you choose to be the energy of in your body? What choice would you choose in what you are creating and expanding all around you in your world? What if true power came by letting go? Especially letting go of the imprisonment of judgment, and the acidic toxicity it creates everywhere.

Let's take a breath...

You can create through the power of releasing judgment and have a whole new life. Experience dropping your walls of defense and feel the space of ease and relax there, make sure you drop them all the way into the core of the earth. When you truly do this the body can rest here, and it's the ahhh space like a fresh breath. Now think of something that triggers you and feel the walls go up. Feel the tension and compression it creates. It's like the fight or flight mechanism kicked in, with minimal space or breath. Which is more familiar and which feels better for possibility for changing anything in your body? In therapies of various modalities, even in CPR the first step is airway (breathing). Compression and contraction take away the breath and there is no "ahhh" space to have any other choice except to lock down.

What if you practice dropping your walls and expand that feeling. Then raise your walls, drop your walls, raise your walls, drop your walls, and etc. Notice the difference by "releasing the power of judgment" you release the walls and have true power of creation of healing with ease, with plenty of space, and with plenty of breath! What would it take for you to choose that now? What would it create in your body and your world by "releasing the power of judgment" NOW? Then enjoy what's beyond!!!

Let's recap...

1. Everything is energy, space, and consciousness (that includes your body).

2. Every thought is energy and accentuated by words and actions.

3. Energy follows your thoughts and what you focus on, you get more of that.

4. Whatever you resist or judge persists and creates a negative response or breakdown.

5. Power is just power and is defined by your thought about it, therefore it can be creative or destructive (especially to the body).

6. Anything is either stuck and rigid or fluid and flexible depending on your point of view.

7. Making a choice can change anything. Change can occur in moments.

8. The body can be a storage dump of judgment and disease or a vital, breathing system of space and power by releasing judgment.

9. Thoughts are transmitted through the nervous system to every cell in the body. All cells have a memory system that affects our health. So what are you thinking?

10. What if the power that is restored from

releasing judgment could change your health, your body, your family, your life, and create with ease anything you desired, WOULD YOU CHOOSE IT?

About the Author

BETH SCHLIEBE

Beth Schliebe is a Certified Access Consciousness® Facilitator, Life Coach, Teacher,

Co-founder of Just Laugh, LLC and Owner of Create Possibilities with Beth for over 30 years. In the past Beth was Co-Owner/ Operator of 18 physical training gym facilities throughout Colorado, Kansas, and Oklahoma. Beth has a joy for life and for helping others. With her business and international training in hands on and hands off energy modalities she uses these practices and expertise's to enhance overall healing though individual therapy, group sessions, as well as creating and teaching seminars. She continually studies the newest possibilities to stay on the leading edge to be resourceful for her clients and family. She is an initiator, motivator, intuitive, and healer choosing to always stay in the question accessing all possibilities that might exist in any situation.

To contact or to learn more about Beth Schliebe:
www.CreatePossibilitiesWithBeth.com.

I would also like to acknowledge these modalities that have been amazing contributions to all aspects of my life...

"Innergetics and Yuen", Dr. Garcia in San Diego

"Access Consciousness", Gary Douglas and Dr. Dain Heer in Houston Texas

"Matrix Energetics", Richard Bartlett in Seattle Washington

Thank you all for the joy and benefits I receive as well as my family, friends, and clients. Also to all on site/remote clients, both two- or four-legged, as well as the earth, and in all my business, we all say Thank you!

Chapter 7

RELEASING JUDGMENT, THE GIFT THAT KEEPS ON GIVING

Laura Hackel

Judging itself isn't good or bad, it is. The more we understand it, the more freedom we have not to let it control out lives.

We all judge. It's part of being human. We look at something or someone and, in less than an instant; we evaluate a situation and make decisions about the person or situation. We decide it's good or bad.

We are conditioned from birth to judge. It started out as a very important survival skill. You needed to judge if you were safe or in harm's way. It has now evolved to a whole new level.

When we are born our family has expectations of what is acceptable behavior. Layer on top of that the expectation our local community has of us, and then, on top of that, layer the social consciousness of a particular topic (children, love, life, works, money). As a result, we have many "unwritten rules" to follow in life.

Imagine that growing up, every time we accepted or agreed to behave in a way that our family, or friends or society expected of us, we were agreeing to put on a coat. Perhaps it was the coat of politeness (when we are, deep inside a "get to the point" type of person), or perhaps it was the coat of not speaking what we see because children should be seen but not heard. We all gather coat after coat as we go through life.

Is it any wonder that at some point we wake up and realize we don't even know who we are anymore?

Releasing judgment is the process to find your way back to your own inner brilliance (taking off coat after coat if it doesn't fit you) and to connect to and embrace the inner brilliance of others.

It requires constant tending and yet, releasing judgment results in freedom from suffering, support for yourself and others, and the ability to live in the flow of life.

Releasing judgment is one of my life lessons. How do I know this? Because every time I find myself judging someone and I don't consciously release that judgment, I have that SAME situation show up in my own life! And, guess what, when it's in my life, I have a whole lot more empathy!

Here's a perfect example of this. Just a few weeks ago, my husband, Evan came home from a weekend of skiing and admitted that he left his laptop in our condo three hours away. I had a field day judging him as "oblivious" and "absent-minded" and even "dumb". Not that he "IS" any of those things, but at the time, it was clear in my head, he was all of them!

Fast forward three weeks later and guess who left their laptop at the condo at the end of vacation week? Yep, that would be me. Suddenly, I had a WHOLE lot more compassion for my husband.

Did I think I was oblivious or absent minded or stupid? Nope, I just thought that I hid it VERY well and so overlooked it while packing.

I am VERY conscious these days when I find myself judging people (and if you are complaining, gossiping or pointing out how you are right, you are JUDGING people, I guarantee it!) that I immediately release the judgment and think or say something to myself like, I know this is happening for a very good reason even if I don't understand it yet.

How do you know you are judging?

How can you recognize when you are judging? You will almost always find a "should" in judgment. Also, if you are complaining or gossiping, you ARE judging.

One of judgment's best friends is drama. When there is drama, you will know that judging is going on. "How could she say that?" or "What was he thinking?" for example. Once drama has been introduced into the situation, our curiosity is out the window and suddenly we feel that we are right and so we actually miss data that is right in front of us.

The Energy of Judgment

I work with energy fields and so I want to share with you what happens to your energy when you are judging.

Imagine outside of your physical body there is a space that is pure energy. It may go three feet all around you or five feet all around you. It may be three feet in some areas or five feet in other areas. We each have a unique energy field that is formed based on our experiences and beliefs. Over time our energy field is filled with thoughts, ideas, judgments, wishes, expectations and experiences.

Some of these experiences are light and airy, and serve us while others, like judgments are heavier, more dense and keep us from vibrating at our highest potential and can also lead to serious health issues.

When you judge others, not only does your energy field constrict, but you are sending others the very real energetic vibration that you do not accept them as they already are. You don't have to say anything; it will be something they feel in the energy. At the same time, judgment causes you to disconnect from people, as you can't be in connection and judging at the same time. This can lead to feelings of isolation.

Judgment's dirty little secret

When you are judging others, you are also, without even realizing it, judging yourself! Perhaps you feel you aren't smart enough, or good enough or worthy enough, you are too fat, too thin, too curvy, too masculine or too feminine. If you don't think you judge yourself first, simply stand in front of a mirror and see what immediately pops into your head.

When you have an unhealed judgment about yourself, the universe magically has it show up all around you. For example, if you aren't comfortable speaking your needs (because good girls don't ask for what they want), occasions where you must speak your needs or they won't get met show up ALL around you.

What I have noticed is, when we judge others, we are really showing that we have areas of us that are trapped inside of us, under all of the coats we have put on in this lifetime, longing to be free.

So while we are wired to judge, releasing judgment (for both yourself and others) and giving yourself permission to be who you really are in the world is the most powerful gift you can

give yourself.
Think about that for a minute.

What don't you accept about yourself?

Why?

Could you write down your three greatest strengths right now?

Could you find three?

How about if I asked you to right down three things that were wrong about you?

Could you stop at three?

I remember very clearly a performance review I had when I was about 27 years old working in a high growth startup company. In the review, 95 percent of it was outstanding and then there was one area that needed improvement. Would it surprise you to know that all of my attention was on the five percent or what I needed to improve and I didn't even REMEMBER what was in the 95 percent? A clear case where I was so focused on what I was judging as bad that I didn't even REMEMBER to take credit for the outstanding bits. Sadly, I am not alone!

So what stops us from releasing judgment?

Often we feel if we accept what is, that it means that we are agreeing with what is. The reality is, when we accept what is, we are free to make new choices that will support us versus being stuck in judgments.

Here's one of my favorite examples. I have three kids and when my boys were 10 and 12, I would pick up the family room each day and invariably there would be parts of gaming equipment or video games or dirty socks on the ground the next day.

It didn't seem to matter how many times I reminded them, I was not able to get them to clean up. You see, in my mind, when they didn't pick up after themselves, I had this whole story going about how they didn't respect me and that they "Should" just be able to pick their stuff up.

As you can imagine, each day I got madder and madder and I lost my cool more than once. I bet you can even imagine the tone of voice I used each time I made a "request" for them to pick up. And yet, their behavior didn't change because I was stuck in judgment.

One day, I got clear that when they didn't pick up it said everything about them and nothing about me. I accepted the fact that they weren't going to pick up each day (after all, they hadn't up until then) and then something really beautiful happened, I got to actually think about, what could I do that would support them picking up after themselves!

After a few minutes of thinking, I instituted a new routine. Anytime I found a cord or plug or game in the living room when I got up in the morning, it was mine for 24 hours. If they wanted it back, they needed to ask me for a chore to do and complete it. Otherwise, they needed to wait.

The first week, I got several "bonus" chores done for me and after that, they got into the habit of putting their stuff away. It took me shifting out of judgment in order to figure out a way to teach them cause and effect. As a bonus, I was no longer angry when I saw their things in the living room in the morning; I was almost gleeful because I knew I could get extra chores done that day.

What in your life is causing you great stress because you are living in judgment? What would it be like to put down the judgment, accept what is and then decide what action you want to take around it?

I invite you to try one or more of these simple techniques to shift yourself out of judgment.

1. If you catch yourself complaining, immediately state three things that you are grateful for at that moment. Then ask yourself, what was your expectation that wasn't met. And then just release it, let it be okay that it wasn't met and decide what choice you will make now.

2. If you catch yourself gossiping, notice it, then let it go, literally feel the energy associated with it moving away from you and know that it is their life, and focus yourself back on your own life. And, if you life isn't interesting enough to focus on, go out a find a way to make it more interesting to you, take a class, go to yoga, or start a new project. Cultivate your interests to make you interesting.

3. If you catch yourself judging someone, stop, take out a napkin or piece of paper or paper plate, and write down everything you know about that is going on in their lives at that moment. Give them grace, affirm that it is NOT about you and let it go.

4. Stay out of the good/bad trap. If someone asks if you had a good day, say "Here are three great things happened to me today".... Or "I had something unsettling happen and I'm still trying to figure out what message I am meant to take from it".

5. When you find yourself judging yourself, name three of your strengths and remind yourself to give yourself grace and permission to embrace all of you. Know that you are already perfect just the way you are. Or, imagine yourself as a baby and send that love to yourself.

What judgment about yourself can you release today that will make you feel lighter and more

alive? Go ahead. Release it!
What judgment about another can you release today that will make you feel more connected and open up more choices for you? Go ahead. Release it!

By releasing judgment, you are providing a fertile ground for your inner brilliance to bloom. Let it bloom fully!

About the Author

LAURA HACKEL

Laura is a #1 bestselling author of the books *"I'm Having It"* and *"The Energy of Healing."* She is a vibrational energy healer and artist, wife, mother of three, writer, and bringer of light to this planet.

She can be found spending her days between her ceramics studio and her healing studio where she delights in helping people make a deeper connection to their soul and the wisdom of their souls and to experience the deep inner wisdom and beauty that exists in the layers, textures and patterns within.

Laura works her magic to help you raise your vibration and live the life you want by using her background as a corporate executive, her Shaman and energy healing training, her intuition and zest for life in general.

One of her favorite ways to clear out stuck energy and bring in high vibrational energy is by playing the crystal bowls for groups and events. Each Bowl is made of quartz crystal and you have lay down and relax as she coaxes beautiful sounds from them that vibrate at the exact frequency you need to first release what it blocking you and then bring in the energy of what you desire. To hear the crystal bowls in action, visit her website at artfulhealings.com.

Laura also makes amazing vibrational Healing Vessels. Each Healing Vessel is formed with her own hands, to facilitate vibrational shifting in both your home and life. There are many shapes and sizes to choose from; each is one of a kind, lovingly handcrafted and sure to shift the energy of any space. Each Healing Vessel is infused with Healing Energy. To select the perfect healing vessel for you, visit artfulhealings.com. You can access her blog and event schedule at artfulhealings.com. Or you can connect on Facebook at Facebook.com/artful.healings.

Chapter 8

How I Judge Me, Let Me Count the Ways

Alex Vogel

"Energy is the currency of the universe. When you 'pay' attention to something, you buy that experience. So when you allow your consciousness to focus on someone or something that annoys you, you feed it your energy, and it reciprocates the experience of being annoyed. Be selective in your focus because your attention feeds the energy of it and keeps it alive. Not just within you, but in the collective consciousness as well."
~ Emily Maroutain

So if that is true what insanity would even possess us to spend even a nanosecond in judgment? How do we stop? Truth, have you ever created change with anything or anyone by doing judgment?

I am so blessed to have an amazing roommate,

Tisha. A few months ago Tisha came home with some agave cuttings and wanted to start them in pots. She asked if I had any pots that she could use. I grabbed a few on the patio that weren't busy and she planted the cuttings. The cuttings happily took to the pots and began to thrive. A few weeks later we had rain, not that common of a thing here in Arizona. Tisha carried the pots out to the front of my townhouse to get a drink of fresh rainwater. The plants never made their way back inside.

These weren't just plain terra cotta pots, these were among some of my favorites. Living in a townhouse, I knew there was a possibility that the pots might grow legs and walk away, being in a common area, or get broken by the groundskeepers. First I told myself Tisha would bring them in soon, when she got around to it. Soon every time I saw the pots in my daily comings and goings I was reminded and irritated. I started judging me for not just letting it go. I began telling myself that it might hurt Tisha's feelings if I asked her to bring the pots back to the patio. No, No, No! I would be in allowance and not let it bother me. The battle went on in my head. Each time I walked past them, usually several times a day, I was reminded to play the loop over again. This went on for over a month.

Then we had a couple of days of frost, this is even more rare than rain here in the desert. Tisha and I were talking about having to clean

off our windshields. It was during that conversation that I finally spoke up for what I
wanted and asked her to bring the pots in so
that they did not get damaged or disappear. I
added that I had never had any frost damage
under my covered patio as if I could assure
that I was not just asking for what I wanted
but was also being thoughtful. She cheerfully
brought the pots back in. Once I actually
asked for what I wanted and saw that it did
not hurt her feelings I began to get how ridiculous the whole story I had built in my head
was. I could see how cleverly I disguised what
I told myself was a kindness to her that was
actually an unkindness of judging me.

I told Tisha how silly I had been. We had a
good laugh and talked about how we create
such insanity. I started by being unwilling to
ask for what I would like. I had to judge me as
undeserving and then judge me as being unkind to hold that in place. Next I had a whole
list of judging how Tisha would react to a request that I had not asked of her. I judged me
for even being concerned about something
happening to the pots, they are just pots for
heaven's sake. I judged me for judging me. I
judged me for being someone who facilitates
clients and students how not create crap like
this, and here I was spinning the loop daily.

The best part came about a week after the
frost. Tisha also had some milk cartons that
had aloe plants in them out front and left them
there when she brought the pots in. One of

them disappeared. I had spent all that time beating myself over the head with my judgment and the whole time it was my intuition telling me that they would get taken. I chose to judge me and deny that I had a knowing. What kind of crazy is that?

We so cleverly do judgment. In many cases we can create a much more elaborate story than this one. We judge ourselves for being bothered by the thing that we are unwilling to ask for. Often people will become angry at the person and punish them for not delivering what they desire even though they never asked for it. Even judge themselves and the other party for how the other person would react if they asked, as if that had already taken place. We create judgment as if it were the national pastime. We are entrained to judge constantly. We judge situations and use our judgment to pretend we have no choice. Judgment is always a lie. STOP the madness!

Most of us start our day with judging our body. Too fat, skinny, saggy, wrinkly, freckled, aged etc. Do you really think your body will be willing to change when you give it such unkind messages? Does it really make sense to expect your body to feel good or healthy when you have nothing but criticism for it?

Sometimes we even do judgment as if it were a contest. One person says, "Oh, I've really got to go on a diet" and the other person says "Oh you think you do, look at me!" That's actually inviting the other person to judge you more than they are judging themselves. Somehow in our heads this is twisted in to being kind to them and saying they don't look so bad, see I look worse. How crazy is that?

We can use judgment to deflect a compliment. Have you ever been a dinner guest where the food was amazing and laid out with beautiful china and serving dishes? When the host is complimented with a thank you for such a fabulous meal, everything was wonderful and then the host says, "Oh, but the gravy was lumpy." It's as if it's wrong or impolite to be complimented, so it must be deflected with some criticism quickly so you won't seem arrogant or stuck up. Somehow we have contorted this in our brain that it's being kind to judge ourselves, rather than receive a compliment. It's certainly not kind to the person giving the compliment to reject their kindness.

We can even use judgment to trick ourselves into thinking that we don't have choice. For example, let's say you choose to go to school. You choose a major. Once you do a semester of classes you see that it's just not a fit for you. You would like to change majors. All the judgments come up of you not choosing the right major. I have spent all this money, so I have to stick with it. What will my family say? Will they say I am lazy, a failure, I don't follow through? Now because I have invested time and money I have to be miserable and end up in a career that doesn't work for me.

What if you didn't judge you as being wrong? What if you were just grateful for the experience? What if instead you just said Hmm, that didn't work out like I thought it would? What can I choose different now? What if you asked, how can I use this to my advantage?

Judgments stop us. They stop us from success, happiness, creativity, relationship and more. They can blind us to choices that are available and have us believing that we have painted ourselves into a corner. I have seen people use judgment to stay in marriages, relationships, careers and so forth that don't work for them. They judge themselves as wrong for making the choice and pretend to have no choice because they chose it.

The fear of judgment is like 'paying' energetically for something that has not happened and may not happen as if it has already taken place. When we operate in the fear of judgment we are being a victim, but we are both the victim and the perpetrator. The fear of judgment invites judgment from others. Being in the victim energy attracts people and situations to become victimized. Being fearful will help you to see more things to be afraid of. Remember we use judgment to stop us. Even if we do the thing we are afraid that someone will judge us for, operating from fear, judgment and victim takes much of our focus and energy and we don't show up as our best self. Then we get really clever here and say see I knew I would be judged, I knew I would mess it up. Then we think we have the proof that we were justified in our judgment and fear.

Sometimes we shrink and become sheepish when we ask someone for something we desire. Sometimes people play small so they can fit someone else's perception of them. Sounds like fun huh? Sometimes showing up small so they don't outshine the other person, so that person can feel better about themselves becomes a habit. Why not shine bright and be the invitation to others to be more?

Know that there is a difference an awareness and judgment. How do you know which one you are doing? Judgment always has an emotional charge; awareness has no charge. You can ask "Is this a judgment or have I become aware of this?"

We sometimes pick up the projections of people's judgments of themselves and believe that they are ours because the judgment is in our head. We are far more sensitive to other people's thoughts, feelings and emotions than we think we are. Have you ever walked into a room and you instantly know that the people in the room are angry at each other, without anything being said. We pick up things energetically all the time. You can just ask, "Who does that belong to? Is this a judgment I am doing or am I picking up a projection of them?"

One of the questions that I use when I find myself judging someone is "Where am I still doing that in my life?" We are easily stirred up emotionally by the very things that remind us of what we dislike about ourselves. When I ask myself this question, I find it easier to be in allowance of the person irritating me and I take a moment for a self-check. If I wasn't judging in this situation, what could I create?

I have not yet mastered being judgment-free, as you can tell from the pot story. I have learned to become more aware of when I am judging and ask questions. I used to spin in judgment of me, and others, a constant loop I would play in my head over and over, looking for all the things to support my judgment or defend against someone's judgment of me. Some loops played for weeks, months and even in some cases, years. Now when I become aware of being in judgment I always congratulate myself. **You see if I berate myself for doing judgment I am just doing more judgment.** I am 'paying' with my energy to create more judgment and attract more to me. How clever, then I can use one judgment to hold another in place.

I have learned to give myself an atta' girl! I saw it and now I can change it. I am grateful to have the awareness of it because I judged for years without even recognizing it. I know that berating me is counter-productive. Judging me as wrong will not allow me to change it. It takes some practice to change the habit of making yourself wrong for doing something that you would like to change. It's 'paying' with your energy to keep you stuck in not changing it. Once you acknowledge something, that is the moment that you have the ability to begin changing it. When you are judging you or reacting to someone's judgment of you, that is giving up your power. Acknowledging it is taking back your power. If you will acknowledge it and own that you created it you can then begin to deconstruct it and make different choices.

There is a magic that happens when you start eliminating judgment of yourself. Others stop judging you. When you are 'paying' with your energy by judging you it's attracting judgment from others. It's like carrying a neon sign that is the invitation for more judgment. Judgments make what you would like to change solid as rock.

When we judge a person it becomes all that we can see about them. You have likely seen this scenario or even participated in it. Two people who have shared a nurturing friendship for years. One of them offends the other one day and from that moment forward they judge everything about the other person as if they have no redeeming quality. All the years of nurturing relationship suddenly have no value. Instead of being an unpleasant incident they become a terrible friend. Some people will even resent any material gift that the other person has ever given them. They use one judgment to hold more judgments in place, often seeking others to agree with their judgments of the person holding even more of the judgment in place. What a crazy way to spend your energetic budget!

Other people's judgments of you are always a reflection of them. We have learned to respond to judgment with hurt feelings, be ashamed, join in with their judgment of us, become angered, and go to defending. When we do this we have made the person judging us more important than ourselves. We become the effect of the judgment and play the victim. We are 'paying' with our energy to make them greater than us. Literally we have decided that their judgment of us is more true and right than what we believe about ourselves. Take a good look at this. Are you willing to give up your power and make someone else greater than you? Is it fun to use their eyes to see you?

Some people actually thrive on the drama surrounding judgment. There is a good chance you know one or more drama/trauma addicts. They take the lead in a dance that they invite you to. They judge you, one, two, you go into defending and explanation (language of victims) three, four, and then you are dancing. Once you take part in the dance you have rewarded the person seeking drama. Many relationships play out these dance steps over and over. The subject may change but it's always the same dance steps. What if you did not react? What if they say one, two and you don't do dance step three, four. What if you just said "Thank you, I had not considered

this. I will look at that." You don't even have
to mean it when you say it. What if you reminded yourself that their judgment was a reflection of them and said to yourself, "Today I
am not giving away my power, thank you very
much."

If you find yourself saying "I don't mean to
judge you about _____ but..." please know
that you are doing judgment. You are saying
that you know more, know better than they do
how to manage their life. What if they are right
where they need to be? What if making what
you see as an obvious mistake is what they
need to choose to push themselves to be miserable enough to choose to change? We give
people advice for what we think will create
something better by our yardstick and we call
it caring and kindness. Some of us even see
ourselves as a rescuer who will save the other
person unhappiness. Really? Does it feel like
caring and kindness when someone gives you
advice that was not asked for? Or does it feel
like they have made themselves superior to
you? If you truly want to practice caring and
kindness wouldn't you choose to 'pay" with
your energy by not focusing on it?

In the TV series Transparent, there is a scene
between an engaged couple. The groom-to-be
had done something to upset the bride-to-be.
He says to her "I don't want to feel like you are
sitting around collecting wrongs, or waiting for
me to fuck up, so you can prove that this relationship is wrong or that you are unlov-

able." This is how we blow things up. We collect all our judgments so we can prove that the job is crappy, or that this is not the right mate for us, or we are unworthy and so on. We collect enough judgments so that we can justify our judgment as being right. We use one judgment to hold more judgment in place.

I worked with a client who came to see me because she hated her job. She thought that our sessions would help her to find a new job that she would like. She hated every moment of being at her job, her supervisor, her duties, her desk, her co-workers etc. She would even get ill before going to work and was missing lots of days.

I asked her to make gratitude lists. Her homework was to write down five things each workday of anything, no matter how small, that she could be grateful for around her job. My co-worker is funny. My desk chair is comfortable. I like doing this part of my tasks. My paycheck allows me to pay the mortgage, eat, and have a car. We have good health benefits. Whatever it was, no matter how small she was to add it to her list. Meanwhile she put out some resumes but she didn't get great response. You see, energetically, she was not that attractive to a new employer. When she had interviews, they just didn't go great.

We also worked with clearing feelings of unworthiness, past failures, and feeling entitled. I have always found where there is low self-esteem there is a false sense of entitlement. We then added homework to do a gratitude list for herself.

As the gratitude collection grew and the judgment collection got smaller, going to work became easier and more pleasant. Feeling sick became less and less. It didn't happen overnight. You see she had built an escrow that she had 'paid' into energetically with her judgment. I encouraged her to take responsibility for creating the unhappiness at the job. I had her ask the questions "How did I create this? If I wasn't telling this story what could I be and what could I create?" I asked her, were other people that worked there that performed the same job she did happy with working there? What was different for them? Gradually she began to see that her judgment of the job had created her discontent and her illnesses. She began to see how she used one judgment to hold more judgments in place. She was always looking for the evidence that her judgment of the job was right and justified. As she shifted from judgment to gratitude, her job evolved into something she really enjoyed. She was offered new responsibilities that were more fun for her and more money. The supervisor that she could not stand became a close friend. She literally became a catalyst for more contentment to her co-workers. You see, judgment and gratitude cannot exist together.

I am continually amazed at how much we can hold in place with our judgment. It is fascinating to me to see in my own life and with my clients that once we let go of our judgments everyone around us changes. We change and then they change. This is the magic of releasing judgment. When we choose to 'pay' energetically with gratitude and allowance we attract gratitude and allowance.

I frequently use one of the tools of Access Consciousness® when someone judges me. When someone is judging, I just say "Interesting point of view, that point of view I have" over and over until the charge goes away. Sometimes it only takes saying it once, for a big charge it may take saying it more.

I have personally played every one of these judgment games myself. Even though I have changed much I still occasionally step back into it. The difference is that I don't sit there long. I have given my body permission to make me aware of when I am judging. My body shows me with a very heavy feeling and a little flutter, like fear. It gets my attention and alerts me to start asking questions. Your body may show you in a different way if you give it permission to show you.

When I ask questions I am not looking for an answer. I am asking for the energy of it, the awareness. Here are some questions and reminders you might use to release judgment.

Give your body permission to let you know when you are doing judgment.

Remember there is a difference between judgment and awareness.

Don't give up your power to those that judge you.

Say no thank you to the dance.

Where am I still doing that in my life?

If I wasn't judging here what could I create?

If I wasn't telling this story what could I create?

To what am I 'paying' with my energy? It is creating more of what I would like?

Praise yourself for catching you doing judgment instead of judging you for it and know that you can change if because you saw it.

Will this create more of what I would like to have in my life?

Gratitude and judgment cannot exist together. Which are you choosing to operate from?

Am I looking for the evidence to support my judgments and proof that I am justified in judging?

Are you being superior or kind?

Interesting point of view I have that point of view I have.

Remind yourself someone's judgment of you is a reflection of them, not you. Am I choosing to be the effect of others?

Am I judging them or picking up their perception of how they see their self?

What could I choose if I were not pretending to not have choice?

Is this a judgment or an awareness?

It is my wish for you that you would look at some of these ways that we can create and invite judgment. Also that you will become aware of where other people are operating from. Do you recognize any of these scenarios in your life? Would you be willing to begin to acknowledge where you are creating judgment of yourself and others? Would you be willing to acknowledge when you are reacting to judgment from others and that you have choice to not be the effect of them? Would you be willing to look at how limiting it is? Would you be willing to become aware of where you are using judgment to stop you from the greatness you could truly be? Would you would be willing to make different choices, willing to take back your power. Remember that when you acknowledge and take ownership for creating it is when you can begin to dismantle the pattern. What possibilities could you create if your energetic budget were spent on gratitude and choice?

ABOUT THE AUTHOR

ALEX VOGEL

Written by Tisha Hoffman

When I first met Alex, I had no idea that we would become friends or the impact she would have in my life. She is the first to compliment you and the last to talk herself up. She has been on a journey much like mine on becoming wholly conscious. Alex enjoys working with people and is THE person to call when you are having what she terms a bad hair day. I know this because she has been the one I turn to when my head gets screwed on backwards. Alex is a certified hypnotherapist, which helps her understand language and how we talk ourselves into a tizzy. Alex presently works for and with her family as the manager and trainer of 10 sales associates. Alex is currently an Access Consciousness® Bars and Body Processes Facilitator. She has had the longest running weekly Bars share in her area lasting four-plus years. Alex has been doing Access Consciousness for five years and says that the tools of Access create change with more ease and speed than any of the other modalities she has tried. She enjoys teaching so much she practically shines from the inside out while facilitating a group. Alex is energized by the excited energy from her students.

From what Alex has told me about her abusive marriage, she could have chosen to be the perpetual victim; instead she chose to be the change. Being the change means embodying what you want to see different in the world. Alex not only creates emotional changes on bad hair days for others, she also creates space for physical changes. An example of physical change is in one of her Access Consciousness Energetic Facelift classes a woman regained 50 percent use of facial muscles after years with Bells Palsy. Another example of physical change Alex had a client with a painful neurological disorder experienced dramatic pain reduction after just one session. Alex has worked with people with cancer and had one client experience spontaneous healing of a skin eruption.

I enjoyed reading Alex's chapter on releasing judgment, it brought new insights beyond what she and I had talked about previously. She has a much broader understanding than what I give her credit for and I am constantly amazed by her awarenesses. I would love to read an entire book written by Alex. It's rumored she is working on about overcoming being a victim. I am personally grateful that Alex has contributed to this book. I eagerly anticipate more from her and the other authors. Erica Glessing is brilliant at gathering contributors for books on subject that change people lives. Alex has been a bartender and a limo driver. Alex is a native Arizonan who loves to knit and is steward to three loving dogs that enjoy meeting new people.

CHAPTER 9

WHAT IF YOUR RIGHT WAY IS THE WRONG WAY?

Keith Grossman

I'm a great leader.

I know how to delegate. I know how to run a meeting. I know how to inspire people around a vision. I spent years accepting leadership positions and learning how to be an effective leader.

I'm truly a great leader; other leaders, however. Not so much.

Putting aside the truth of the statement (meaning: maybe I'm not as great as I think I am), I have a tendency to judge others by my own standards. I especially judge by my standards people who are taking over a leadership position from me. Of course, judging in that situation is natural to do.

Years ago, I finished my term as president of an organization, and I attempted to counsel the new president. I wanted to see him succeed, and I knew I had all the answers. I suggested he delegate a number of tasks to the paid staff and hold them accountable. I encouraged him to develop relationships with all of his Board members and communicate with them regularly. I explained to him the value of asking Board members to discuss even the smaller, inconsequential decisions so that they felt ownership over the organization and wanted to participate more.

The new president ignored all of my advice. He didn't have enough time to do these things. He didn't feel decisions needed to be made "by consensus". Involving too many people just slowed everything down. I was surprised by his response. He seemed so... so... cavalier... about his leadership. Did he actually want the organization to be successful?

Regardless of whether my advice was truly sound or not, I thought my advice was good advice, and the new president's contradictory perspective resulted in me forming judgments about him. He was taking the organization that I worked hard to build and grow stronger, and he was flushing it down the toilet. What a terrible leader!

When the volunteers complained to me that they weren't clear on their responsibilities, I questioned the new president whether he had a problem. When the staff and Board members complained to me that communication was horrible, I hinted to the new president that he had a problem. When Board members told me they were no longer part of the decision making process, I told the new president he had a problem.

I realized, though, I was only looking at the situation from one perspective — my own. Everything was black and white to me, and whatever he was thinking, was black and white to him. I really needed to release judgment and understand his perspective. Maybe some of his ways were better under the circumstances. Maybe we could come up with better solutions together than we could by ourselves. I was emotionally attached to "I am right", and my energy was destructive.

I stopped sharing my concerns with the new president. Instead, I supported him for his efforts. When he asked the Board for input on a decision, I told him it was a good idea. When he shared information with the paid staff, I told him I'm sure they appreciated hearing the information from him. The result? He became a little more flexible in this thinking and came to me more frequently for advice.

Releasing Judgment

An effective leader delegates and transfers leadership responsibilities with support and without judgment. The other leader is different, not wrong. My judgments were preventing me from growing as an individual and preventing the organization from growing as a team.

I was preventing the organization from bene-fiting from our cumulative knowledge, experi-ence, and passion.

Judgment was invented by society. It is all about measuring what is right and what is wrong, and what is right and wrong is based on our own standards. Does the other person measure up to our standards?

Judging others is a mental activity. Our brains produce thoughts. We then interpret those thoughts and apply meaning to them. We de-cide how attached we are to those thoughts, and whether we will use them to measure oth-ers.

By judging another person, we are making that person "wrong". They should "be" or "do" the way we want them. We are standing in a place of superiority and deeming them to be infe-rior. We then start the process of correcting them, blaming them, and condemning them. These are all attempts to control, convince, and change the other person.

People don't like to be judged because we are typically judging them by a different measure-ment, a different set of rules, than their own. People being judged usually become defen-sive because nobody wants to believe they are "wrong". The defensiveness can lead to rebel-lion and retaliation.

People only willingly accept judgment from

people who they believe share and support their own values.

The additional problem with judgment is that we fail to communicate and work together effectively.

- Ordering and demanding causes fear, resentment, and anger.
- Warning and threatening causes fear, resentment, and anger.
- Moralizing and preaching causes guilt.
- Lecturing causes feelings of inferiority and inadequacy.
- Shaming and ridiculing causes guilt, inferiority, and inadequacy.

The good news is that you can release judgment of others. It isn't easy. There are benefits to releasing judgment, however.

- Improved relationships
- Increased commitment to follow through
- Creative problem solving

Opinions are not Judgments

It is fine to have different opinions. Opinions are not judgments. Opinions are your personal feelings you have on a subject. They are snapshots in time, and you are allowed to change your opinions as you explore new information.

If you don't allow your opinions to change, and you hold onto them as if they are irrefutable truth, your opinions become inflexible judgments.

You can share your opinions for the basis for persuading others. Once you share your opinion, however, let it go. Don't judge the person who disagrees and doesn't act consistent with your opinion. Let go of convincing, correcting, controlling, and trying to change others.

Understanding another's perspective

"Before I can walk in another's shoes, I must first remove my own." - Unknown

In order to release judgment, you have to be open to understanding the other person's perspective. You have to see things from their point of view. Our judgments of others tend to be skewed. We don't know how the other person journeyed to where they are in life - how they make decisions; how they behave.

Steven Covey made this idea widely popular when he taught that one of the 7 habits of highly effective people is to "seek first to understand, then to be understood". It's opposite of what we normally do, which is to listen from our own perspective instead of the perspective of the speaker. We are caught in our own little world, and we're not paying close enough attention to the wants, needs, and interests (WNI's) of the other person.

I one time ordered a veggie sandwich as take-out from the local deli. The menu listed a variety of vegetables that came on the sandwich. As the employee was making the sandwich, he looked over and asked, "What do you want on it?" I figured he meant in addition to all the yummy veggies listed on the menu.

I answered, "You can add lettuce and tomato."

"That's it?" he responded. What I heard was, "No mustard or mayo?"

When I got back to my office and opened the packaging, I discovered I had a sandwich consisting of lettuce and tomato on wheat.

I cursed the fool, but the reality is we had a total lack of communication because we both approached the event from our different perspectives. I assumed he was familiar with and followed the restaurant's menu. He assumed I was creating my own sandwich from scratch.

A common reaction to something another person says or does (or doesn't say or do) is to make assumptions about their motive. Typically, we attribute a negative meaning to their behavior. We then develop a response based on a set of faulty, negative assumptions lacking a clear understanding.

The employee probably thought I was crazy for

only wanting lettuce and tomato, and I certainly thought at first that the sandwich symbolized what a moron he was.

Neither one of us was wrong. We were measuring each other by a different set of expectations. Understanding that allowed me to quickly change my opinion and release my anger.

A friend of mine told me a story about when she started a college program to become a physical therapist. On the first day, the professor facilitated with them the following exercise.

Imagine that you are on a subway train in New York. There is a man standing up who is all messy and disheveled. He smells, and he is falling asleep.

The professor then asks the students, "What are your impressions of this person?"

Of course, the students listed out some impressions similar to what most people would think. The man is a bum; he is homeless; he has a drinking problem; he has a drug problem.

Are the students observing everything, though? Are they actively looking for the bigger picture? What are they missing and not noticing?

Maybe this man just worked three straight shifts to make money to support his family.

Maybe he is actually diabetic and suffering from diabetic shock. Maybe his wife recently died.

A failure to understand the man's perspective is a failure to understand.

Understanding another person's perspective is hard work. It's worth the time, though, because:

- it provides clarity to the challenge.
- it opens minds to greater options for solutions.
- the other person feels respected and valued (and even loved).
- it provides greater credibility to proposed solutions

Wanting to understand the other person is a way of saying "I'll open my mind for YOU".

Tolerance

We all bring to our relationships our complete backgrounds, including childhood experiences, education, religious beliefs, and values. Tolerance is the ability to accept others for their differences.

David Gauthier, a Professor of Philosophy, offers this definition of tolerance: "A willingness to allow, without endorsing, the ways or objectives or values of others, and to be willing to interact with them without seeking to change their ways and values, while following different ways and holding different values ourselves."

Walter Isaacson, the author of biographies about Benjamin Franklin, Albert Einstein, and Steve Jobs, has talked about tolerance as one of the traits of genius. Isaacson says Ben Franklin possessed the quality of tolerance. "He understood if you create a society with great diversity and everyone is tolerant, it will be stronger."

Tolerance doesn't rely upon shared affections or friendship. It further doesn't rely upon shared objectives or advantages. Tolerance represents the idea that people can interact in ways that furthers the different objectives of each person.

Intolerance can cause stress and conflict, so tolerance has a direct relationship to wellness and life satisfaction. Unfortunately, many institutions inadvertently promote intolerance—if you don't conform to our way of thinking, we will take some negative action.

People have to get comfortable with the idea that accepting someone else's differences is not agreeing with them. You can accept the other person's different perspective, different way of doing things, etc. without getting upset about it. Life's experiences continuously show us there is usually more than one way to accomplish something. Accepting that somebody has a different way does not signal your approval.

Tolerance can be more than acceptance, however. True tolerance means recognizing the value in our differences. Without differences, our world would be unattractive and boring. Tolerance allows us to celebrate differences and grow stronger together as a direct result of those differences.

With tolerance comes humility and the ability to humble yourself to other peoples' opinions. "Most creativity comes from a group of people who play off each other, who cover each others' weaknesses, and amplify each others' strengths," Isaacson says. "Over and over again, you see Franklin's wisdom, which is bringing people together. That's part of his genius."

Here are some tips for achieving tolerance:

- Be curious and open-minded to learning about those differences and encouraging those differences.
- Admire the differences and imperfection in each other.
- Be courageously authentic and honest with each other.

How to Release Judgment

Reframe judgment with validating statements:

For example, going back to my story about the incoming president, instead of saying "What a terrible leader", I could remind myself "Progress and change take time and patience. I choose to be patient and compassionate through the process".

Reframe judgment by analyzing actual consequences: For example, instead of thinking the incoming president is destroying and undermining our previous efforts, I could recognize that we just need to take a different path to achieve the outcome we all desire.

Reframe judgment by observing how you can grow as a person and obtain a deeper appreciation of others: For example, instead of negatively labeling the incoming president's methods, I could look closely to identify positive results due to his different methods. I could then learn how to apply those same methods myself.

If you find yourself judging someone, think about how much you disliked your crotchety grandmother complaining you slouch, you chew gum too loud, and/or your hair is too long. You didn't like it, and nobody else does. Make a commitment to release your judgments. When we let go of our "right" way and the other person's "wrong" way, a shift can happen towards a relationship where we can seek to understand, share, teach, and help each other.

About the Author

KEITH GROSSMAN

 Keith Grossman helps individuals and businesses negotiate and manage conflict more comfortably.

Keith is a Collaborative Attorney, a Family and Circuit Civil mediator certified by the Supreme Court of Florida, an Arbitrator qualified by the Florida Supreme Court, and an educator. He works with teams and with individuals one-on-one helping improve collaborative and negotiation skills and strategies.

Keith helps you "think outside the court" so you don't go broke and you preserve your relationships. In fact, the Lee County Association of Family Law Professionals awarded Keith the 2015 Hugh E. Starnes "Think Outside the Box" award for leadership, critical thinking, innovation, and dedication to non-adversarial practice.

Keith has frequently lectured and facilitated training programs and has written articles on conflict management and consensus building topics. He also is the writer of the blog ResolvingConflictsNow.com.

His e-workbooks, "What Is A Peace Chest?" and "How Do You Build A Peace Chest?" are available on Kindle.

Keith graduated from the University of Florida with a law degree as well as a Bachelor of Science in Journalism. He is a Past President of the Lee County Bar Association, as well as a member of the Collaborative Professionals of Southwest Florida and Society for Human Resource Management.

CHAPTER 10

NOTHING LEFT TO BE EXPECTED

Carol Glover

It was so natural I didn't even know I was doing it: judgment. I was so good at it that I could judge myself, what I was or wasn't doing, I would judge others, and I would judge others for judging me. That's a lot of judgment going on — completely unconsciously.

In fact, I spent a good portion of my life so caught up in being, doing, or saying the right thing that for a short time I took medication to cope with keeping up the ruse. It seems every fiber of my being was clamoring to be heard. The more I created the life I was supposed to have, the more my spirit screamed for something different.

It was a little like going into my sister's closet and putting on her clothes. They're not quite my style and certainly not a great fit, but I could "make do" if they made me feel a little closer to fitting in, even if I was uncomfortable. I was wearing a life that didn't quite fit; my relationships, my work, my home, and my spirit were all uncomfortable. And yet, somehow, even in all of that, I wasn't completely unhappy. I was uncomfortable and knew there had to be more.

For me, 2003 was the big shake up year. It seems the entire Universe had enough of my judgments creating my life and was taking matters into its own hands. I was restructured out of my career and chose out of my home and the relationship that came with it. Within a matter of months I was in a new place with a completely blank life in front of me; there was nothing left to be expected of me or by me. And in all of that I was more comfortable with me than I had ever been.

Perhaps I should clarify what I mean by comfort here. We've all been told that you have to take big risks, big leaps, stretch yourself, think outside the box and get outside of your comfort zone to get anywhere in this world. How's that working for you? I can tell you that all it did for me was make me incredibly uncomfortable and it made me feel like a failure, like I was never doing anything right, like I never fit anywhere and that I could never possibly have the things that I desired.

Getting back into your comfort zone is not about never challenging yourself, it's not about never allowing yourself to grow or expand. In fact it's the exact opposite; it's about learning to trust your knowing. It's knowing where to stretch yourself and when rather than taking everyone else's advice about where, when, how and why. You already know what you desire or require and how to have it. We're just trained not to believe we know.

It's about not using this largely messed up world as a measuring stick of what you are or are not, what you're doing or not doing. Those are somebody else's rules, and we don't really know if they work for the people that made them up. It's about knowing that there's a uniqueness in you that requires your own expression rather than making yourself a poor duplicate of someone else. It's about coming to the place of honoring yourself and creating your own version of reality with confidence, even if people think you're crazy.

It's only when you are comfortable and using your own knowing that you are able to be a full expression of you. If you're operating from the place of judgment and trying to fit into everyone else's expectations, it's less likely that you're going to be able to do or be what that the world requires. We need more people being brilliant! We need more grown-ups remembering they are brilliant. We need you to remember and be as brilliant as you were when you were eight years old and knew everything.

It was only when I began to listen to myself and my own knowing that things started to fall into place and judgment started to lose its grip on my life. I'm not saying life is perfect yet, but it is so much sweeter, so much more fun and I love it when I do things my way rather than the "proper" way.

Now, back to the story...

The next several years are a bit of a blur as I went about creating my new life, there were bumps and some possibly not great choices made along the way but all in all, I was much more comfortable with and in my life. By 2006 I was married to a brilliant man and by 2009 I was building my second business.

I began guiding people in managing and growing their businesses by honoring their nature and their knowing. As we worked together, I could see who they were beyond who or what they were trying to be and I could sense their vision. Together we would clarify that vision and find simple ways to bring it to fruition.

Oddly, it wasn't often that they chose to follow the simple/easy way. Not only did that seem insane to me, it frustrated me beyond measure until I remembered that it was their choice. It did however leave a shadow of doubt in me about my knowing. Could I really be so delusional to think that business could be easy when it was clear that most people are operating from the "hard work" and "fight for success" point of view?

It was easy for me to get out of judgment of my clients — not so much for myself. Still, I knew business and ease can co-exist and I was spending thousands of dollars on courses and experts trying to figure out how I could sell it. It's hilarious to me now that I was making ease so complicated, not judging (but probably judging) my clients for not choosing it, and not choosing it for myself either. Again the Universe stepped in; my own business was crumbling. Again there was nothing left to be expected of me or by me. This time, I was shown my true knowing in two short conversations.

The first was over a cup of tea with a local social media expert. We met through Facebook and thought we'd get together and get to know each other. During our conversation, she asked me a question: "If you knew, when you were starting out, what you know now, what would you do differently?"

My answer came without hesitation "I would have followed my own advice. I would have taken all of the information that I received from all my training and I would have tweaked it to work for me. And I would have done that a lot sooner rather than thinking the experts must have successful businesses doing what I was wanting, to do so I'd just copy them."

As soon as she asked me that question, and I realized how easy it was for me to answer without hesitation I knew! I knew that while wishing I would have tweaked everything to work for me, I could choose to do that now!

Two days later I was sitting with my coach, having another one of those days where I was stuck and struggling. I was unsure of what to do with the awareness from the other day. My coach asked, "Carol, if your business fails are you a failure?" DING! DING! DING! Of course my answer was NO! I'm still smart. I still have all my knowledge. I still have an amazing heart that desires to support people to find their version of happy or brilliant or whatever it is they seek. I could NEVER really fail at anything AND I can choose to change anything at any time!

Those two questions in such close proximity reminded me of my knowing and prompted me to choose back into following it again. My entire business changed within two weeks. I quickly and easily dissolved a partnership I had gotten into that wasn't working, and I shattered the template business model I was trying to stuff my creation into. I created an extended services contract with one client whose business continues to bring me absolute joy and that in turn – as if by magic – has created so much flexibility and room for expansion in my business and in virtually every other area of my life too.

I feel like a magnet for magic now! Getting out of all the judgment of how I *should* be doing my business, where I *should* show up to get clients and what I *should* say when I get there, has made all the difference. Following my knowing and choosing things that match the energy of what I desire to create has made all the difference.

Since judgment no longer plays the leading role in my life, my business isn't the only thing that's benefited. My relationship with my husband was great before and now it's off the charts wonderful! In fact all of my relationships are easier. I'm so much more grateful for all of the gifts this life and planet has to give me, right down to the wonder of a sunrise, the touch of a raindrop or a smile from a stranger. Without judgment life becomes more about inviting the world in and being present with it. It's an affluent, wondrous, magical way to exist.

There is one side effect that may be a little uncomfortable at first: you may no longer wish to hide yourself from the world. When you are operating from your knowing, you are not leery of presenting yourself in the world. You are not leery because you know what is required from you (and for you) in every moment.

If you're operating from judgment you will always find yourself lacking and you will either physically hide from the world or you will be SO "out there" and yet not showing the world any of the real you – you're hiding in plain sight so to speak. You're likely constantly exhausted by continuing to strive to cover up the real you and do the expected.

Removing judgment, following your knowing,

being in your comfort zone leads you to be completely present in all situations, no matter how awkward they may be. You'll be the one standing confidently in your life and exclaiming things like "This is who I am, I may not be everybody's flavor, but I'm not going to hide anymore!"

In following your knowing, you find that your will is stronger, you are more capable, more empowered and simply freakin' fantastic really. You start to get more comfortable with your life and all the different aspects of it – even the so called crappy bits. You may even find that people come to respect, appreciate, and value you and your "differentness" more than ever before. Life becomes more exciting and easy.

One of the things I struggled with most after discovering just how prevalent judgment is in my life, was deciphering whether a thought was judgment, or knowing. For me, it's a difference in energy: a judgment will feel like a hard stop whereas a knowing seems to be more open. With a judgment, there's no place else to go. With a knowing, you have information that can lead you to making choices.

Have I eliminated judgment from my life? Not likely but I am able to sense the difference in the energy when I'm in judgment and I can make a change on the spot. Was it easy to switch to following my knowing? Heck NO! Not at first anyway, and certainly not when it meant I'd have to speak up about something or make a choice that may not look popular, practical or logical.

At first, I had myself convinced that my knowing must be wrong – a lot. I had the impression that I couldn't possibly know anything that the rest of the world didn't already know. I thought that if everyone else knew what I know and they weren't using that knowledge, then I must be wrong or at least the information was not of any value. I must be wrong – UGH! More judgment! Does it ever end?!

Thankfully, there did come a point when I realized that the way I was operating was exhausting and frankly it just wasn't working to build the life I desired and knew was possible. I really had nothing to lose by at least experimenting with choosing based on my knowing. It wasn't always comfortable (sometimes it still isn't) and yet I know it will create anything I desire.

I've come to realize that judgment was put in place for many reasons, not the least of which being that it keeps us in control and it keeps us buying what industries have to sell. I've also discovered that judgment and my knowing cannot occupy the same space at the same time.

I now know that my knowing can present itself to me many ways. Knowing can come from a thought dropping into my awareness, from a conversation over a cup of tea, from a bird at my bird feeder, or from a child. Really, my knowing can come to me from anywhere, and I'm so glad it does!

Something in me knows that I can't go wrong following my knowing. I know that I can be, have, do or create anything I desire if I listen to and follow my knowing. And I'm pretty sure that the universe is happy knowing that it won't have to scramble my entire life to get my attention when I slip.

Now that I've stepped back into choosing with my knowing, I'm much more comfortable, much more productive, and much more creative in all aspects of my life. I'm excited to see what happens next and I'm confident that me and my knowing will do wonderfully!

About the Author

CAROL GLOVER

 Carol is an Author, Radio Show Host, Business Advisor, Business Energy Reader, Access Consciousness® Bars & Body Process Facilitator, and so much more!

Carol has her Project Management Professional designation and over 20 years of intense corporate experience in which she has developed a keen ability to meet business challenges with elegant solutions. In 2009 she founded FireHorse Consulting Inc. and continues to use all of her capacities to bring ease to the businesses and lives of her clients through it.

In early 2013 she discovered that she was able to bring her personal studies in consciousness and Universal Energies directly to businesses with profound effect. Upon recognizing that each business has its own energy, she was led to bring the healing arts directly to her client's businesses. The results of this work have ranged from subtle to remarkable and continue to astound and enliven her as much as her clients. Carol now brings her Business Energy Infusions to her private clients and in regular group settings, bringing ease to businesses just as effectively as she does to bodies.

In addition, Carol enjoys sharing her clumsy explorations of self and business through her Radio show "Clumsy Girl's Guide to Greatness" as well as through her writing and speaking engagements.

www.carolglover.ca
www.firehorseinc.ca

CHAPTER 11

THE JOURNEY BEYOND JUDGMENT

Kim Cooper

It was 1994, and I was about to leave the relative security of the college campus I had called home for the last five years. I had accepted what I thought would be my first real flying job. In South Carolina. Where I knew no one.

I had been offered a job as a flight instructor by a woman who ran a flight school. I was already flight instructing, but the irresistible carrot she dangled in front of my nose was the opportunity to build the coveted and hard to come by multi-engine time required to become an airline pilot. She promised I would be flying a Beech Baron for a client who kept his airplane at her airport. Little did I know that the client had no intention of replacing his current pilot. The woman I went to work for didn't like the current pilot and wanted him replaced.

Long story short, I ended up moving miles away from home and everything I knew, into what seemed like a completely foreign culture to me, to take a job that I already had.

I grew up in Pittsburgh, a working class town that never met a stranger. People smile at each other on the street and say hello, whether they know you or not. When I left home to attend Purdue University's aviation program, I wasn't lonely for long. I was surrounded by many other freshmen in the same boat, all of us eager to make friends, set our own curfews and make our own rules.

I thrived in college, out from under the watchful eyes of my parents for the first time. I loved being a member of a select group, about 40 students out of a campus of thousands, who were learning how to fly airplanes. My friends headed to English Lit class, while my classroom was the sky.

I realize now how much I craved being acknowledged; the surprised look on people's faces when I told them I was learning how to fly, the reverence I was shown later in life when people asked what I did for a living and found out I was an airline pilot.

I arrived in Greenville, SC in the spring of 1994 at the age of 22; before the BMW plant arrived to give the town it's more cosmopolitan, international vibe. I had never been to the south before.

Other than one trip to Florida, and another to Canada as a child, my parents stayed pretty close to home and rarely ventured more than one state away from the security of their roots. Quite ironically my father hated to fly, only stepping foot on an airplane for the trip to Florida, his hunting trips to Canada, and one flight with me when I graduated from college. I don't know what happened on the hunting trips, but on the other two flights he gripped the seat in front of him or my mother's arm with all his might, as if he were willing himself to stay alive just one more day. I never understood his fear of flying, or how I developed my wanderlust and desire to travel to foreign lands.

South Carolina opened her sweltering arms to me with an oppressive heat and humidity I had never experienced before. Afternoon thunderstorms barreled over the mountains every afternoon with a vengeance, disappearing moments later as quickly as they had appeared.

As if the assault of the soaring temperatures on my sweat glands weren't enough, my taste buds were in for a surprise as well. Growing up as the descendants of German immigrants, my family had meat, potato and a vegetable for every meal. My father's idea of foreign food was anything that strayed farther than spaghetti; I never experienced anything like Indian or Thai cuisine until I was married. It took me a while to become accustomed to the food of the south – the bland grits, the collards I had never heard of, the vinegar-based Carolina barbecue, and the delectable indulgence of sweet tea.

I found the people of South Carolina an enigma, as difficult to figure out or predict as the afternoon weather. Some were incredibly friendly, some acted as if the Civil War had just ended yesterday and I didn't belong. All were equally difficult for my Northern ears to understand.

I ended up spending the next 11 years in the South — always a Yankee to the locals, and yet my friends and family back home continuously made fun of me for the southern accent I had acquired. I felt like a stranger in a strange land no matter where I went, not quite fitting in, in the North anymore, not yet assimilated into the slow drawl of the South.

My first trip out of the states as a pilot was to the Bahamas. I was flying a cargo airplane, and we were supposed to deliver our load and just stay long enough to get some rest and head back home. We coerced our boss into letting us stay a few extra hours, so we could partake of some rum punch, conch fritters and a head full of braids for me. That trip made me realize how much I loved experiencing other cultures: the smells, the food, the customs, the religion, and the people.

The people of South Carolina weren't so impressed with my Bahamian braids. As I traveled around the state dropping off midnight loads of cargo at small airports, I was at the receiving end of quite a few quizzical looks, and a few souls were brave enough to ask what I had been thinking. I started wearing a hat to work, and was grateful not many people milled about the airport in the middle of the night. I was less enamored with the braids myself a few weeks later; on a slow day at work I spent hours unwrapping them, and later ended up with an unwanted haircut to remediate the damaged ends.

My time in Greenville and that first trip to the Bahamas were my first taste of the diversity available to me through travel. Since then I have explored many countries, the most memorable being: Jamaica, Poland, Czech Republic, Austria, Italy, Holland, France and the United Kingdom. After each visit to a foreign land, be it the Deep South or the Swiss Alps, I return home a different person, forever changed by the experience. Renewed by the people and the culture. The world is a melting pot, filled with more offerings than I could partake of in a single lifetime.

I've often tried to pinpoint exactly what it is I love about traveling, and the one thing I keep coming back to is the diversity. Everything is different in a foreign country, and it is the difference that I find so captivating. Each corner exposes something new to be experienced, and an opportunity to connect with people who look and sound vastly different to me, and yet in many ways are surprisingly the same.

One of the things that drew me to becoming a pilot was the uniformity required for the job, so the realization that I enjoyed things being different came as a surprise to me. After all, I chose a career where we not only dress identically; we repeat the exact same terminology flight after flight when reading our checklists. Standardization is paramount, so that at any moment one pilot can be replaced with another and we all know exactly what to expect.

Being known as a pilot held a certain reverence for me, and became my identity. I played my role perfectly, never daring to do anything that would make me stand out or appear too different. Never straying from the well-respected, reliable, trustworthy, straight-laced stereotype I had in my head of the perfect pilot. Which is ironic in its own way.

Conjure up the image of an airline pilot in your head. Is it a pretty young female, or a wizened, white-haired, mustachioed old man? All the time I thought I was blending in, yet I was already standing out. I even declined the female tie offered as an alternative to the standard uniform, preferring to wear the male-issued tie so that I would "blend in." Considering how much I loved being around people that were different, it was amazing how hard I tried to be the same as my male crewmembers.

I WAS different, no matter how desperately I tried to be the same. My fear of being judged by others was huge, but not as huge as the hefty amount of self-judgment I served up daily to myself like a big, fat, juicy steak. I was juggling a job as an Airline Pilot, nurturing a fledgling business, and taking care of my family, and I still never felt like I was "enough." My unattainable goal was to be all things to all people, and that belief kept me perpetually dissatisfied with myself, no matter how much I managed to accomplish.

Although I judged myself all the time, I was immobilized by the fear of being judged by others. I was especially concerned about being seen as weird or different. It was almost as if I were trying to clear my own "faults" out of the way before anyone else had a chance to discover them. And of course, I was much more unkind to myself than anyone else ever would have been.

And yet somewhere, deep down beyond the fear of judgment, beyond the false belief that I could ever "judge myself into being a better person," I had the desire to be different.

In my late 30s I was introduced to a group of people whom I immediately resonated with; a group of friends who were so unlike the ex-military, Midwestern Christian Conservative, middle-aged men I was surrounded by at work. This group of friends wore tie-dye and dreadlocks and played music. They spent their Friday nights at drum circles. They chanted things like Om Mani Padme Hum and were into self-help and alternative healing. More than ever before, I felt like I fit in without even trying. I had found "my people." Not only did they not judge me, I didn't judge myself when I was around them.

I spent a weekend with my new friends at a retreat and had a fabulous time. The only downside was I spent the entire weekend terrified that someone would post a picture of me on Facebook.

What was I afraid of? That people would see me dancing? Drumming? Standing next to a barefoot hippie in tie-dye with a smile as wide as Detroit?

I was afraid of the judgment. I was afraid of being the girl with the Bahamian braids again. Instead of embracing the diversity within myself that I found so appealing in the rest of the world, I felt I had to fit into either one box or the other. The Pilot or the Bohemian. Either/or, there was no room for "and." I gave myself no allowance for "different."

I'd like to admit that I was able to change things right there and then. That my desire to be different and "authentically me" overrode my desire to "fit in" and not be judged, but that didn't happen. Instead, I spent the next several years leading two separate lives. My upper middle class, white-collared pilot life, and my bohemian, free-flowing, alternative healer life.

It wasn't until I found the tools of Access Consciousness® in my early 40s that I began to comprehend the possibility that I could have ALL of me, without having to divorce parts and pieces of myself to "fit in." For the first time, I heard someone say that judgment wasn't real.

What? How could that be true? If judgment wasn't real then why had I wasted so much time and energy trying to avoid it?

Let me say it again, in case it has scrambled your brain as it did mine the first time I heard it – JUDGMENT ISN'T REAL. It's someone else's interesting point of view and nothing more (or it could also be your point of view about yourself.) You don't have to buy it as real or true. You don't have to agree with it. And you don't have to resist or react to it.

Over the next year I began to integrate my two personas. I cautiously began to talk about Reiki and Essential Oils in the cockpit; I stopped hiding that I was a pilot when I was staffing a transformational retreat. I became an Access Consciousness Certified Facilitator and started guiding others on the journey of self-acceptance. I stopped wondering, or even caring, if people thought I was weird.

One of the greatest joys of being a facilitator is watching the ah-ha moment that occurs when someone decides to choose possibilities instead of limitations. I'm so grateful to be present when a client finally chooses to break down their walls, uncover their magic and show the world ALL of their gifts and talents.

After 26 years of flying, I left my airline pilot job in October of 2015. I moved on for many reasons – I had twins on December 31, 2014, and no longer had the desire to spend half of their lives away on the road, as I had done with my nine-year-old son. I had a business that wanted to grow and clients asking for change, and not enough time to nurture or guide them between my travel schedule and my family. I knew I had more to offer the world than just flying people home for Thanksgiving. There were plenty of pilots capable of doing that job. Only I could be me.

JUDGMENT ISN'T REAL

If judgment isn't real, how much energy are you wasting worrying about it? Who could you BE if you stopped judging yourself? What could you accomplish if you weren't worried about being judged? What could you create in your life if you let go of the judgment, and embraced whatever it is that's waiting for you on the other side?

Is now the time?

Journey on my friends. Journey on...

About the Author

KIM COOPER

I'm a Facilitator, Writer, Magic Maker, Worldwide Creator at Pathfinder Healing Arts, Mom of three precocious boys and a former Airline Pilot. I'm also a lot of things that aren't easily described by a title or in a few words. That's one of the reasons I changed the name of my website from Pathfinder Healing Arts to Being Kim Cooper, a continual reminder to myself to BE ALL of me, all of the time.

Throughout my life, I wasted a huge amount of time and energy trying to "get it right." Which meant that I vehemently tried to avoid being wrong. Or judged. Or weird. Or different. Now, instead of worrying about criticism or judgment or trying to avoid confrontation at all costs, I realize that the opinion of other people is just their own interesting point of view, and it's my choice whether I decide to buy it as real and true. I teach my clients and class participants how to stop fearing judgment and do the same. I accompany them on their journey as they rediscover their magic, and embrace all they have to offer the world.

As an Access Consciousness Certified Facilitator, I guide people on an exploration to discover the areas of their lives where they are limiting themselves. With my arsenal of practical tools and bodywork experience, I show my clients how to release their limitations and create the future based on new possibilities, rather than trying to create from outdated beliefs and judgments of the past. Clients then have the opportunity to create a future beyond what they might even imagine is possible.

Here's a testimonial posted on my Facebook group from my most recent client –

> "If it's time, whatever you do please contact Kim for facilitation. She knocked about 50 years of programming of fear and judgment out of me. WOWSERS!!!!!! In so much gratitude of you Kim. Thank you for the gift that you be!"
> ~ J.W – Ontario, Canada

What gifts and talents do you have to offer the world? Who could you BE if you allowed yourself to release judgment? Is now the time?

I currently reside in Pittsburgh, Pennsylvania with my husband and three sons, but the world is my playground and I love venturing out into it and all it has to offer. I am available for classes and facilitation worldwide, in person or via Skype.

I wonder what kind of magic we can create together?

Website
www.BeingKimCooper.com

E-mail
kim@beingkimcooper.com

Facebook
www.facebook.com/beingkimcooper

CHAPTER 12

RELEASING JUDGMENT: BEING YOUR TRUE ESSENCE

Linda S. Evans

I awoke one morning about a month ago with a promise to myself to avoid all judgment of anything, anybody and myself. I was well-intentioned and feeling clear and conscious. Within five minutes, I noticed at least 10 judgments pass through my awareness. I noticed a few wrinkles on my face, an additional bulge in my waist that wasn't there before the holidays, and a few new grey hairs on my head. I was judging my beautiful loving cat for desiring to go outside before I was ready to open the door and set her free to make her morning rounds.

I cringed as I observed the mess around the fireplace, which was a natural result of the beautiful warmth the fire had provided for our home during the night. I judged the clutter beneath the Christmas tree with the dead pine needles falling to the floor, just following the natural laws of gravity. I then became aware of how I was condemning myself for being so judgmental despite my good intentions.

I was feeling frustrated by how deeply ingrained we all are with this judgmental game, even among those who consider themselves "spiritual" and "conscious." How did this judgment habit become so embedded in the bedrock of our culture? Variations of this painful judgment game seem to hide in the core cellular level of our bodies and vibrate in the mysterious caverns in our minds. That morning, I became acutely aware of the insanity of the energy of judgment. How crazy is it to judge the result of the natural flow of life? Cats want outside every morning to explore their territory. Wood turns into ash when burned. Leaves and needles fall from trees in the natural evolution of life. We often feel quite justified and rational with our judgmental perspective and we give logical reasons and explanations as to why something should not be the way it is. I wonder how insane we are making ourselves in thinking things should be different than they are?

There are so many types of judgments pervading our society. Just reflecting about the holidays, people judge how well they shop, if their gifts are "good enough," if their holiday meal is better or worse than last year's. We obsess about if we are eating too much and gaining weight during the holidays. As we get together with our beloved families, we judge if we or they are in better health, looking older, making more or less money, living in better or worse homes, driving fancier cars, taking the best vacations, giving the most to the best charities. We make comparisons about whose children are going to the best colleges or becoming most happy and successful. We judge the parenting skills, volunteer projects, alcohol and medication use. We often even judge our own and others spiritual practices. Most of these judgments are not spoken out loud in front of each other. Most are whispered quietly when you don't think they will hear or the next day in a phone conversation. Though most of us don't enjoy these thoughts and concepts, it is hard to escape these themes, as they just seem to come up from inside of us – like a ghostly monster that can't be seen, found or captured and killed. It's frequently rearing its ugly head. Perhaps this is why so many people dread holiday gatherings as they sink in the quick sand of judgment and the comparison game and miss out on the potential magic and miracles of the special season.

Holidays just seem to highlight and amplify these judgment games. These games are happening every day of our lives. Most people don't enjoy these energies or seek them, however, most people are the effect of them every day in their families, homes, careers, schools, recreational activities and even churches.

Unraveling the judgment cycle with the people with whom we live and love is often a challenge. I have been married for 22 years to a most wonderful partner, lover, friend, father to my children and spiritual soul mate. Yet, I still find myself judging when he doesn't do what I expected or desired that he do. For example, I can quickly fall into judgment when he leaves his dirty socks on the floor or doesn't complete a household repair as quickly as I desire. Finding some amusement when these crazy-making judgments arise has been the key to unlocking the prison of judgment and creating a relationship of love, respect, and freedom to express our own selves authentically.

Even more challenging has been the arena of parenting. Parents desire the very best for their children. In our attempts to insure they are happy, safe and growing into their highest potential, it is easy for our opinions and ideas about what is best for them to interfere with the free will of our children and their freedom to create their lives the way they desire. Schools are rampant with "comparisonitis." Some of this may be considered healthy and inspiring to children to do their best. Some of it is quite unhealthy and wounding to the hearts and souls, especially if one has a 'different' way of learning or 'different' gifts and talents. Many parents attempt to force their children into extracurricular activities, which they feel are good for them rather than what the children are actually interested in or where their interests and talents lie. That rarely lasts long or goes very well. For me, I judged my son harshly at age 16 when it became apparent that he was choosing not to focus on his schoolwork and healthy after-school activities. Instead of my desires for him, he found new friends, with other less-than-healthy interests, in my opinion. I informed him how terrible this was, how it would affect him for the rest of his life, attempted to scare him with the potential dangers of his choices. None of this changed his mind. My judgments only pushed him away from me. I was not free (or sane) until I released all judgments I had about these choices he was making. It was only after choosing to let go of all judgments were we able to communicate and enjoy and appreciate each other again.

Additionally, I judged my daughter's cancer as bad and myself as a bad mother for choosing to have a daughter who chose this painful experience with cancer. How crazy insane is that? I was a 'bad' mother for having a daughter with cancer. I was a 'bad' mother because my daughter was diagnosed with malnutrition when undergoing chemotherapy. There were many bad mother associations in that experience. However, I know I am not alone. I hear many mothers judging themselves every day for situations with their children, which are clearly out of their control.

I was not able to heal or let go of any of that painful experience until I realized how deeply I had judged myself and had some awareness about the decisions I had made about myself as a result of those judgments. I had decided all my spiritual tools and information were worthless, as they didn't work to achieve the outcome I desired. I had decided I had been abandoned by the Divine since the outcome was not as I preferred. I had decided that I had been wasting my time and money on spiritual trainings as nothing was working. You see how all these decisions I made as a result of my incorrect judgments kept moving me further and further away from the truth of what was really happening. That is how judgments operate – they clump together into hodge-podges of conclusions and decisions, which move you further away from yourself, your freedom and choice. Once I honored my daughter and the spiritual choices that were all coming together in this transformational experience for all of us, I was free of judgment, and I surrendered into the serenity, peace and expansiveness of what was unfolding.

While judging family members, friends, and colleagues is pervasive, self-judgment is truly the most difficult habit to stop. When we are in judgment of ourselves, we feel guilty, unhappy, anxious, blocked creatively and tend to self medicate. In my experience, I have noticed three most common judgment themes:

1. There's something wrong with me
2. I am not worthy – not deserving
3. I am not good enough

Imagine with me for a few minutes. What might the world look like, feel like, be like if we were all free from these core concepts of wrongness, unworthiness and lack? I see a peaceful world of plenty, joy, and freedom. Bringing it back to yourself, what if you experienced a whole day without those vibrations of wrongness, unworthiness and lack? Feel into it and notice your beautiful smile in your heart and soul. I choose that reality!

How do we break free from this? Being free from this pattern of judgment is the key to unlocking our happiness and expressing ourselves freely and fully. When we are in that vibration of our own highest creative expression, then we are also in allowance of all other people in our lives to be free to be themselves and choose whatever they desire.

Being in judgment is being stuck in a non-creative vibration. Energy stops moving literally when it is in judgment. We become stuck in a "no-choice" universe when we are in judgment. It's important to stop stopping yourself by being in judgment. Analyzing, justifying, defending, and making excuses for judgment just keeps it more stuck and turns it from glue to concrete. In contrast, if we move about in our world with perceptions or awareness, we are gathering the information we need to keep moving forward without making judgments or decisions which cut us off from this space of awareness and perceiving. One of the best ways to get unstuck from judgment is to ask a question in the vibration of wonderment. Ask a question like "I wonder what else is possible?" This gets the energy moving. This literally opens up your space, your mind, your universe to other possibilities that you could not be aware of when you were stuck in the judgment energy. It creates a doorway where before there was just a barrier or a wall. You go through that doorway and you have new vibrations to perceive and then you can ask another question to open up another doorway to another possibility. There are infinite possible alternative universes which you can approach simply by asking questions. Asking questions is like keeping the propeller of your awareness and perceptions moving and creating.

Judging is like adding glue to your propeller and each judgment, opinion, decision, conclusion adds more glue to the propeller until it can no longer rotate around anymore. Your universe, your plane, your helicopter is landed and stuck in judgment. You are not able to move or go anywhere. Start asking questions, the propeller starts spinning, blowing off the glue and you are moving again on your own adventure in space. Questions are literally the fuel that keeps you moving.

Our primitive brain, programmed to make judgments, decisions and to survive wants to categorize everything into good or bad, right or wrong, helpful or hurtful, happy or sad. All these categorizations were required for survival at some points on our sojourn. These concepts are programmed in the core of our body as survival information. Now, we no longer need this programming to survive. As we love, pamper, nurture our bodies, we let our bodies know that we are no longer being threatened.

We are living in safe places with plenty of food and we no longer have to worry about survival. As we tone down this primitive survival part of our brain, we can activate the right side of own brain and tap into our creative juices. As these creative juices flow, alternate realities open up as possibilities and become available to us. New realities that we never knew were possible become possible. We make friends who don't judge and compete. We have bosses who perceive how great we are and we don't need evaluations. We enjoy watching our children, partners, friends and colleagues blossom into their full potential.

To be free, it can be helpful to look at how judgment became so deeply ingrained in our cultures, minds, emotions, bodies, and habits. How does it persist despite so many awesome potent teachers like Buddha and Jesus who clearly demonstrated and taught followers not to judge, and gave many examples of the re-percussions of remaining stuck in judgment? I see the persistence and density of this vibration of judgment goes back to the archetypal story from the Garden of Eden when the choice was made to partake of the tree of knowledge of good and evil resulting in our "fall from grace." For the first time, there was separation, there were negative thoughts and feelings like "evil," shame and embarrassment requiring us to cover ourselves with leaves and hide. Note that it doesn't really matter whether you believe in this story or not. This story is an archetypal part of the foundation of life on this planet and this awareness is part of cracking the lock on the prison of judgment in which we are encaged.

As we become aware of the "original sin" vibration, and remember the energy of free will and the vibration of our original likeness and image of God, then we can begin to free ourselves from this prison of wrongness. Once we are more conscious of this cage of wrongness and shame, we remember that this is not our truth as we are all "sparks" of divine, actually with all qualities of the divine, then we can KNOW the truth of our original essence and this lock of wrongness falls away and we are free from the prison of judgment.

So, as you read this now, take a deep breath and acknowledge yourself as an infinite eternal being, made in the likeness and image of the Creator or Source or Divine or whatever name you like. Know that you are vibrating in this essence of your true nature and from this vibration, everything unlike your true essence falls away. There is nothing wrong with you and you are free from that original judgment of something was wrong with you or that you had done something wrong. Forgive yourself and all others you have encountered along your journey for having forgotten your true nature which is love. Congratulations! You are breaking free from this bedrock foundation of wrongness. You are starting to get your free will back. You are free to vibrate in your original true essence which is Love and Light. You can make a different choice from this point forward. Are you willing to move forward in this vibration of choice, awareness and freedom?

I like to remember that all judgment is a lie. No matter how certain we are that our judgment is true, it is important to remember if we want to be free of the chains and restrictions of judgment, we must know that whatever the judgment is, it is not true. It is a misperception, a lie, an illusion. This is the easiest way to let it go, let it dissolve, let it dissipate in knowing that there is no truth to it. Don't engage in argument about it, just know that it is impossible for it to be true. It is OK if others around you believe it to be true. Don't try to change their mind. Just settle into your own essence of alignment with Source, God, Divine truth and essence.

I also like to remember myself as a child of the Light of truth. From that vibration, I am illumined by the light where there can be no judgment. People in our lives are just showing us where we are still stuck in judgment and giving us opportunities to clear all judgments, opinions, decisions, conclusions. In the heart there is no judgment, as there is only love and there is only oneness. If we focus on creating our lives from our hearts where we are one with everyone and one with Source, we will experience less of this painful judgment.

From Judgment to Choice

Looking at these specific areas has helped me to release judgment from my universe:

Body

We look in the mirror and our eyes usually go to the "worst" parts of our bodies – the fat stomach, sagging breasts, cellulite in the buttocks are just a few common examples. The more we do this, the more disconnected we become from our bodies. The more disconnected we become from our bodies, the more disembodied we are. This results in the bodies shutting down and becoming much more likely to become ill. If we love and appreciate our bodies, look for the beautiful aspects, then the beautiful aspects expand and we find ourselves in loving communication with our bodies, adoring them, asking them what they desire and giving them what they desire. Our health is vibrant and we exude wellness, joy, peace, love, adoration and people feel those vibrations when they are around us and we are a blessing to all with whom we interact.

Mind

Many of us carry the thoughts that we received from our parents, teachers, religious leaders regarding our "role" in society, our religious beliefs, our political beliefs, how to live, what to eat, what cars to drive, where to live. Many of us follow this leadership from our parents and teachers or rebel and do the opposite. Either way, we are not functioning from choice. We are becoming the effect of these thoughts, beliefs and emotions as we learned while growing up either by following their footsteps or rebelling at the opposite end of the spectrum. To set yourself free, release and let go of all these debates, issues, and conflicts and drop into your heart where you know you are love and light and let that vibration expand into your whole body and mind. Let the peace of your heart quiet your mind and know that the truth will set you free.

Heart

Generally, the heart is very non-judgmental and loving unconditionally. That is the natural state of the heart – loving unconditionally. It is vibrating in the oneness of all things. It is through the heart that our oneness with the Creator and each other is felt. What will sometimes block this easy flow is the heart wounds. Perhaps you felt rejected or unloved or abused by a parent or a lover, the heart is wounded and barriers go up. As barriers go up to protect oneself, then the flow of unconditional love is also blocked. Judgments of who is safe to be around and who is not safe serve to hold up the barriers and protection. Let go of all judgments knowing that they are a lie and are only hurting yourself. Drop all armor, barriers and walls and connect to your oneness with the Divine. Know you are safe in this vibration of love and light and it is the truth of your being.

Allow this to heal all heart wounds and bathe in the vibration of your own true essence.

Soul

As a spark off the divine, you have everything the creator has as well as all the aspects of the creator. This is you vibrating in your true essence – in the image and likeness of the divine with all the same qualities and potential capabilities. As a soul on a journey, we have all had many lifetimes where we have gotten further away from this original essence as we experimented with our free will, made choices and learned about the consequences and repercussions of theses choices we have made. I believe that's why we continue to take bodies and incarnate, so that we can gather ourselves up into the wholeness of ourselves, forgive ourselves, gather our energy and information so we can be more conscious creators. So, we are all journeying back to our oneness with the Divine Creator Source Energy. The more conscious we become of this, the less we desire to create separation, the less we judge as we know judgment is creating separation.

3 Step Process:
To Release Judgment and Be Free

1. Awareness

Make a list of all the judgments that you have of yourself and others. Take some time to write it all down without judgment. Let yourself let it all out. Remembering that most judgments stem from a sense of wrongness. Prompt yourself with starters like:

I judge myself for...

I hate....

I can't do anything right like....

I can't stand...

I will never be able to do the things I want to do because.....

I am too old to......

After giving yourself plenty of time to write these judgments down, tear all these papers up and burn them in a safe container. Let all the energy stuck in these concepts release from your body and dissipate as the papers burn. Give yourself total permission to let all this go and make a choice to create from a vibration that is free of all this judgment and comparison energy. Know the truth that all these concepts are false concepts/lies with no real basis.

2. Imagine

Picture yourself free from all these judgments. Imagine yourself at about six or seven years old playing free from all adult opinions.

What would you be wearing? What would you be seeing where you live?

What would you be saying? What would you be hearing?

What would you be singing? Dancing? Painting?

What would you be smelling?

What would you be tasting?

Ask yourself: what would bring you the greatest joy? Imagine it. Draw it. Be it!

See yourself enjoying your creative juices flowing.

Feel yourself in the energy of your highest creative essence.

Be who you really desire to be. Act it all out and have fun doing so. Really let yourself play.

Give yourself permission to play every day in this vibration of you. You will notice it becoming a part of your every day creations.

3. **Surrender**

Now that you have this concept that it is possible to be judgment-free, surrender into it. Imagine there is an energy bubble in front of you and step into it. Imagine your heart, mind, body and soul all integrated and stepping into this full awareness of yourself as an eternal infinite being made in the image and likeness of the Divine. Be that vibration.

Feel into it on a deep cellular level in your body. Feel it washing through and in all the cells of your body – down your arms and legs, through your heart and abdomen. Feel it washing through your mind, your brain, balancing out the left and right hemispheres of your brain. Feel it in the energy field around your body, your aura. Feel it in your connection to the Mother Earth and Father Sky.

Align all these energy fields together and know the truth of your being which sets you free.

While there are many different spiritual paths, most are designed to facilitate people on the path of making their way back to our fully conscious creative nature in alignment with the Divine Source Creator. In our true divine nature, there is no judgment. That is what we all yearn for and dream of. We make commitments to function from that original essence vibration, yet it continuously challenges us. Is it the impossible dream? Is it possible to be truly functioning in our every day lives without this toxic vibration of judgment? I do believe it is possible and imperative for our continuing life, growth and expansion on planet earth. This is the time for all of us to experience heaven on earth. This surely must require that we sweep all judgment from the earth and release it from all hearts, minds, bodies and souls. This is your invitation to be free from all judgment, choose yourself, choose love and light, choose life as it was meant to be, choose a slice of heaven today.

About the Author

LINDA S. EVANS

Linda S. Evans, MA, has worked in health care as a Certified Nurse Midwife since 1994. She considers it an honor and privilege to have welcomed over 2,000 babies into this world. Providing a safe physical space and holding an energetic welcome for souls to enter new bodies has infused her with appreciation, admiration and adoration for all souls who choose to incarnate into this beautiful planet Earth.

Additionally, Linda has taught meditation and energy healing specializing in women's intuition and self-healing since 1991. In 1999 Linda and her husband, Don, founded a sanctuary for the celebration of spirit called The Earth and Sky Church. In that setting, they provide energy counseling, meditation and self-healing classes with the primary goal of creating a safe space for people to learn about who they are as spiritual beings. The training they offer allows students to discover their own gifts and talents, empowering them to bring their gifts to the world.

Linda is currently providing coaching and inspirational speaking to facilitate people to live fully alive. Linda dreams of a peaceful world where all human beings are free to express themselves fully, joyously, authentically and receive their hearts desires.

If you would like transformational coaching or would like Linda to speak at your inspirational event, contact her at linda@fullyaliveliving. com or visit www.fullyaliveliving.com.

CHAPTER 13

HEALING CANCER, HEALING LIFE

Smriti Shivdasani

"I am happy, loved, respected and supported. I am grateful for me and I feel blessed."

These are words I could not have said a few years ago. My story, for the most part of my life, was that I felt unloved, abandoned, abused and I was definitely not good enough and smart enough. Little did I know that this story would unravel and gradually change into something beautiful because of one diagnosis that would shake up my world, my entire existence so far.

In 2012 I was diagnosed with breast cancer. I had already lost my mom to cancer in 2004 and I went on to lose my father to cancer in 2013. I had to look at life really closely. What was it that was creating so much cancer in my world? I knew that there was something I had to change within me to change this outside of me. We are the creators of everything, after all. So what was it that I had to change? I truly believe that beyond every hardship there is some amazing potential waiting to be unleashed. The hardship is just a catalyst to reveal that gift which, in turn, can be a contribution to humanity. What could I create now from this business of cancer that could serve humanity?

As I prayed with this question in my heart I was led to alternate healing. That set me on a different journey altogether, a journey I now share with all seeking to change their lives. I wish someone had taught me as a child:

- My thoughts, emotions affect the energy flows in my body and that an imbalance in those flows leads to disease.
- My points of views, belief systems create my reality.
- I am the creator of my reality. No one else is responsible.
- There is greatness in each of us waiting to be revealed.

And so I began my journey. I had to see for myself who I was being. I was bitter and angry about so many things in my life. I was a prisoner of millions of judgments and I was a fantastic drama queen. I felt abandoned when I had to go to study at a boarding school at the age of 10.

I tried to commit suicide at the age of 14 when I felt so alone, humiliated and so judged by people over a few unpleasant incidents in school.

Sitting on top of the building, I couldn't get myself to jump. Ha! I couldn't even do that well.

Blaming others for my unhappiness became my mantra in life. I wasn't aware how that judgment "No one loves me and I am not good enough," created my world as I saw it. And so, life kept getting created similarly as I grew up. Disastrous relationships were all I had, some horribly violent too. Ending my life seemed to be the only option sometimes. I came close to it another couple of times but never had the guts to go through with it. In hindsight am I glad I didn't give up on me. It was not lack of guts but a knowing that there is more to me than I am aware of that kept me going.

Now, as I faced everything I was being with complete vulnerability, I knew I was the creator of my own reality. I could not blame anyone anymore. Being a victim would create nothing joyful for me. The healing process had begun.

I faced all my wounds, anger, rage and bitterness using various healing modalities I learned. The Cancer had to end... beyond surgery and radiation. It had to end in the depths of my life. The anger, hatred, fury, rage, judgments, bitterness and everything else that held cancer in place had to be released. There was no other way. This I knew now. I cannot explain how I was so sure about this being THE WAY to heal. All I can say was that I JUST KNEW. It was a very slow process until one day when I got to an Access Consciousness® class called "Access Bars". It was an answer to my prayers. Gary Douglas, the amazing man who has founded Access Consciousness, explains what judgment, both positive and negative, does to our life. We cut off our awareness of everything else, each time we come to a conclusion/judgment. We can only receive that which matches our judgment. When I heard him say "your point of view creates your reality" my world just opened up. My point of view, my conclusion, my judgment that I am not good enough and that no one loves me had created my life as just that. My life was partnering me to reflect my judgments about how mean people were, how selfish, how they take advantage etcetera, etcetera... My points of view were creating my reality. This had to change. The blame games had to stop. The judgments had to go.

I started using Access tools to destroy and uncreate all the judgments I had. Yes, you can actually destroy and uncreate them at will and change your reality. Here is how:

Interesting Point of View (IPOV)

One of the tools that worked brilliantly for me was "Interesting point of view". All of us look at the same thing but each of us has a different point of view and hence it looks different to each of us. Hence, no one's point of view is either wrong or right. It's just a point of view. How much of my life had I created defending the rightness of my point of view? How much pain had I created justifying how wrong people were when they said or did something to me? As I looked at my life, my choices and the judgments as just an interesting point of view, the guilt, shame, regrets, anger started falling away. There was nothing wrong with me or my choices. They were just interesting choices. Those judgments that made me feel horrible were just interesting points of views. And so, I started to set myself free from all the judgments I had about me and also those I had bought from others about me. I can now look back and actually laugh at all those interesting choices and points of views.

Anytime you catch yourself judging yourself or someone else OR if someone is pushing their judgment of you onto you, you can just look at it and say to yourself "Interesting point of you that I have this point of view". You may not believe it initially and there may be plenty of emotional charge but as you will keep saying this, the charge dissolves. I invite you to try it and play with it.

Consciousness

In my Access Bars Class manual, consciousness is explained as follows:

"Consciousness is the ability to be present in your life in every moment, without judgment of you or anyone else. It is the ability to receive everything, reject nothing, and create everything you desire in life – greater than what you currently have, and more than what you can imagine."

~ Gary Douglas

Wow... this was precisely what I required. Observing my life from this perspective of consciousness was like entering a maze made up of innumerous walls of judgments. How much of these walls prevented me from receiving all of me and life itself? We are always happy to receive the good and the beautiful, but what about the bad and the ugly? Could I have so much allowance in my life and receive everything without judgment?

What about those people who were mean and abusive?

What about the times I felt cheated?

What about the times I failed?

What about the times I could not stand up for myself?

What about the time I was slapped and humiliated in front of a whole dormitory of girls for no fault of mine?

What about the times I was punished just because some secret admirers sent me love letters?

What about the times when I just couldn't get maths and statistics, physics and chemistry, and did not do well?

The list was endless. But I could do it. I looked at all the judgments I had about the events and the people involved and blasted those walls till I emerged in the open space where I was free and happy. I also became present to the awareness of what is meant by the age old saying "What you resist persists." How much energy was I giving to all those people and situations with my judgments and my resistance to them? I was not willing to receive the bad and the ugly. I was resisting it and putting up walls with my judgments. While I may have gotten a temporary relief doing that, what I did not realize was that those same walls were preventing all the good and the beautiful from coming into my universe too. I could only receive what matched my judgments... the bad and the ugly. Was it any wonder that I was solidifying similar situations again and again in my life? Besides IPOV, what empowered me to blast these walls of judgment was the following tool.

Judgment Process

I was watching a Google hangout by Dr. Dain Heer, Co-founder of Access Consciousness and author of this gorgeous life-changing book called *Being You, Changing the World*. What I am about to say is my interpretation, and not his exact words. What he said was to the effect that we cannot judge anything that we ourselves have not been or done before. Woah!!! Did that mean that everything that triggered me into irritation, anger etc. was something I had done sometime in this or some other life-time? I had to look at so many judgments once again, and run the judgment process that he explained on that hangout.

I saw what triggered me... one at a time... I saw how I judged people when I got triggered and I went... "Everywhere I have been there or done that I now destroy and uncreate it. Right and wrong, good and bad, pod and poc, all nine, shorts, boys and beyonds." These words may sound strange but they are the magic wand that blasts all the limitations we have created in our world. Called the Clearing Statement, it has been explained beautifully by Dr. Dain Heer on www.theclearingstatement.com. The clearing statement is designed to bring up en-ergies and clear them. As we think of the sit-uation that is triggering us, there is an energy of it that becomes present along with all the unconsciousness and points of views etc. that have created this situation as a limitation in our life. That which we create unconscious-ness about keeps us stuck in the part of re-ality we are looking to change. The clearing statement erases all of those energies without having to know when and how and why we created the limitation in the first place.

Needless to say I was running this process all the time. So many judgments!!!! And I was wondering why my life was the way it was!!!!!!! Really??? My typical day went like this:

I am driving and someone cuts in and I go

"What the *****." OK so everywhere I have been such a driver...

My husband is behaving a certain way and I catch myself getting irritated. Ok. Stop. So what is my judgment of him in this situation? Hmm. Interesting point of view I have this point of view. And everywhere I have been there or done that...

I have gone shopping for clothes and I catch myself judging my body... nothing new, but this time I stop and say "Interesting point of view that I have this point of view about my body."

I hear from a friend and realize she is still stuck in her drama and trauma. My first impulse is to tell her to stop like I have always told her and then I go... NO. It's an interesting choice that she is making. She must love it for some reason to choose it again and again. I know she can be happier if she would change, but is she willing right now? And so I clear all my points of views I have about how she should change and I get on with my day.

I get to know that someone, whom I thought was a dear friend, was talking mean things about me behind my back and it really hurt. After wallowing in hurt for a while I decide to stop. Everywhere, across lifetimes I have done that to others, I now destroy and uncreate.

I read an article of something that has happened in the world somewhere and I catch myself getting very judgmental about the people involved I go... Wow. Everywhere I have invoked or perpetrated that across lifetimes...

I see some stranger behaving a certain way in a public place. My first response is "How can that person be like that or behave like that?" Miss Judgments is up and about once again. Hmmm, interesting that I am being so judgmental. Everywhere I have been that or done that...

And so it went. Being present in every moment is not exactly easy. You get to see who you are being and not all of it is very pleasant. However, if you can see it and receive it all without any judgments you get to a better place soon enough where you can love you and accept you unconditionally.

In this lifetime I may have never done that or been that which I judge in this moment. But I have lived many lifetimes and done everything, been everywhere and hence when I see it in my universe now, I get triggered by it. Would you have an opinion or judgment of something that you have never ever experienced before? Just asking. I invite you to look at what triggers you and see what points of views and judgments you have about that person or situation. You will see how those points of views are creating your reality.

However, one word of caution, being in allowance of what is, receiving everything and rejecting nothing does not mean you have to be a doormat. It's not like anyone can do anything to you and get away with it while you go "Interesting point of view." So here is another tool to use alongside the other tools.

Awareness

You always have an awareness of what works for you. I invite you to honor that awareness. I am aware when a person is simply mean by nature and that's just the way that person is. Or if someone loves drama and I have that awareness that that's just the way that person is. There is no judgment in my universe of that person. That's just their way of functioning in life. However, I am also aware when their being that way doesn't work for me. So I refuse to allow someone to be mean to me or beat me up or be abusive or allow myself to be dragged into their dramas. I see what I need to do to that is nurturing for me and I do that. If it means keeping my distance I do that. This kind of awareness also empowers me to be in allowance of all that is.

There are so many other tools in my kit bag that I could share. However, for now all I can say is that releasing judgments is magical. It transforms your life like nothing else does. Nothing outside of you can change without first changing within. It could be a tiny thing like making up your mind to stand up for yourself or to do something to honor or nurture yourself or this massive journey of looking at yourself in all honesty and with complete lack of judgment and going ahead and releasing all judgments and points of views you have been imprisoned by. It is like de-cluttering the inner cupboard. It has freed up so much space in my heart that my life feels lighter. There is a sense of peace in my world, joy in my heart. I get out of bed looking forward to the day. It's not just any other day. My relationships are nothing short of being beautiful. I can actually talk to people and receive them without judgments. Everything and everyone is just a point of view. If I had to ask you to spend your day with:

A) someone who judges you and criticizes you without bothering to find out how that makes you feel

B) someone who indulges you, loves you just the way you are

Whom would you like to hang out with ? I bet you answered B.

And that's how it is. I would like to hang out where I am not judged. What would our world be like if each of us were in allowance of all that is and did what was honoring of ourselves and others. Wouldn't it be a different world where existence would be peaceful and joyous?

And so I decided to use one other huge tool called CHOICE.

Choice

If there is one thing that is freely available to me it is CHOICE. The choice – to be a certain way, to judge or to not judge, to be happy or miserable, to be courageous or defeated – is always mine. It is also my choice to have no choice. I chose to become someone who is free of judgments no matter what it takes. It is a constant practice to be aware of my choices and what they create in my world. But I am getting there. This inner transformation has created much beauty in my life.

One of the biggest blessings was the way this journey transformed my relationship with my husband and our daughter. As I released my judgments I had of them, and believe me there were many, I became an energy that invited them to choose something different for themselves. Both of them also started using some of the tools and running bars. I feel grateful for who we have become as a family. My life long dream of being loved and cherished for who I am has come true. How does it get any better than that? Yes that is a question you can ask whenever something good or bad happens to you and the universe can't wait to show you how. Ask and you shall receive.

And so my journey continues. I went on to attend various Access Consciousness workshops and became an Access Consciousness Certified Facilitator. I facilitate various kinds of workshops empowering people to see and be the greatness they truly be. I am so grateful for all the blessings I receive from participants and clients.

It's a magical existence. Can I say that I have arrived? No. Each day I discover judgments that I have not seen before and I clear them. Each day creates more freedom for me. There is no judgment of my judgments anymore and that's a great place to start each day. Interesting point of view I have this point of view is what I say when I see myself judging. And I run the judgment process. It's fun to see where all I have been across lifetimes and what all have I done.

I am grateful to you dear Universe for being the mirror that shows me everything that I am, that reflects all my points of views and gives me life each day to polish the mirror of my life. Thank you for having my back. I am free.

"I am happy, loved, respected and supported. Everything I desired as a 14-year-old child sitting on top of the building finding the courage to jump to death (or live perhaps). Today I am grateful for me and I feel blessed."

And so it is.

May you discover the greatness you are and the joy that your life is.
God bless.

Smriti

ABOUT THE AUTHOR

SMRITI SHIVDASANI

If one had to use few words to describe Smriti, fondly called Smi by her friends, they would be versatile, dynamic and determined. Over years she has worn many hats, experimented with life and explored who she is. She has been a beautician, banker, a real estate and relocation consultant, a jewelry and home accessories designer and in her own words has now come home, doing what she believes she was born to do... to empower people to be who they truly are... to be happy.

Her life's journey has not been easy. Growing up as a bitter and angry child and then an unhappy adult she tried giving up on life a few times. However, her determination to change it all, her conviction that there is more to life than unhappiness, there is something great out there waiting to be claimed, led her on the path of life. Little did she know that a disease called Cancer would set her in that direction that she sought.

Her experience with cancer, first losing her mother to it, then going through it herself and then losing her father to it has led her to explore alternate healing and life management skills. Smriti's journey into facilitation first began when in 2012, she had an epiphany. She was guided to offer meditation classes. Having no clue what was to be done, she followed that guidance and invited her friends to her first meditation class. There has been no looking back since then. Those sessions have gone on to become guided journeys. In her one hour sessions she and her participants explore things such as offering gratitude for everything that comes into their awareness, offering energies to all seeking it, exploring areas in their lives where they can bring hope where there is despair, light where there is darkness. Then there are sessions where they explore the greatness which lies within each of them and seeing it in everyone.

She has, since then, gone on to learn various modalities such as Reiki, NLP, EFT, Matrix Reimprinting, Past life regression, Jin Shin Jyutsu, Angel therapy, Crystal healing, Cell Regeneration, to name a few. She added facilitation of self-help workshops using EFT and Jin Shin jyutsu to her repertoire. Another turning point in this exploration and learning came when she attended her first Access Bars Class in 2013. There has been no looking back since then. Access Consciousness tools are her favorite. She is constantly having fun attending Access Consciousness classes herself, keeping abreast with the latest processes and also facilitating various Access classes as a Certified Access Consciousness Facilitator.

Her tagline says it all: "Empowering you to be the Greatness you truly be." Her determination is to share her joy of being empowered with people from all walks of life, individuals and corporates, and equip them with easy to use tools to transform their health, money, business and relationships.

She is her own source of happiness and joy. She enjoys being the Creator of her life and has eased off her old role of being a Drama Queen. She can be reached at:
smriti.shivdasani@gmail.com.

CHAPTER 14

CREATING BOD-EASE WITHOUT JUDGMENT: A JOURNEY WITH TEENS

Julie Oreson Perkins

with her teens, Connor and Christy

Attention! Calling all Bodies! And Bod-EASE! Is now the time to create EASE with your body? In whatever way that looks like for you? What do **you** desire with your body? More energy? Less pain? What else? What if releasing judgment of YOU *and* YOUR BODY is the key to creating your life and your body with EASE? Take a moment to become really present – to be "here and now" – with your body. Now take another moment. And one more. And one more still. Plus another one. What did you notice as you really focused on – and with – your body? I often start my coaching sessions this way, especially if a client is experiencing a "dis" of some kind: dis-comfort, dis-content, dis-approval, dis-connection, dis-couragement, dis-combobulation, dis-harmony and even dis-ease. Why? Because I have learned (not always the easy way) that excluding your body from the equation of your life creates dis-ease.

That's where my adventure – and the journey with my teens and all our bodies (Bod-EASE!) began... with the dis-ease. We've spent a good amount of time exploring this, looking at what's underneath all the dis-ease with our bodies. And what did we find? A MASSIVE mound of judgment! Here are some highlights...

Secrets and Lies

Looking back now, I can see that one of my first disconnects with my body happened when I received "the talk" in health class about "becoming a woman" biologically. I remember feeling the embarrassment (or was it shame?) of that "secret visitor" that came to young girls my age – and how I thought that meant "leave your childhood behind" because it was "time to grow up." I recall thinking, "Ugh, I don't want to grow up and say goodbye to fun. This seems *so* serious." I even had visions of flying off to Neverland and staying young and playful with Peter Pan. The whole thing just didn't feel like *me*.

Body biology changes = a monthly "curse to endure" for the coming decades. **(Gulp)** That was the first big "body" lie that I swallowed. It wasn't until much later that I realized just how much I had separated from my body because of that – nor did I notice how much of what I was experiencing at the time was really my awareness of all the other girls' expectations, conclusions and judgments about what this time of life *should* mean.

Fast forward several years. I am in and out of intimate relationships. One of them is a "secret one" with a guy that I am "not supposed to be with." We are very connected to each other physically, emotionally and spiritually... until he decides that I don't "fit the profile" of what his ideal woman looks like. I wasn't tall and leggy enough – blond enough – skinny enough.

(*Gulp*) I swallowed all that too, like a fish biting a hook with squirmy worms of secrets and lies. More separation between my body and me. And again, no recognition of that until much later on.

What did all of this create for me? It contributed to bouts of dis-ease over the subsequent years including: anxiety, high stress, no sense of self, breast cancer and severe adrenal fatigue (with the latter two occurring while I was a mom of two young kids.) I was "sick and tired" of being "sick and tired" and struggling to keep my head above water each day.

Family Inheritance

Fast forward again. I have begun a spiritual journey to "find myself" because I feel "lost." Our kids are now "tweens" and I'm being the "good parent" and providing them all the "right" information about bodies. Their dad joins the discussions and adds what he knows about science and medicine and bodies. Since he's a Reiki master, he talks about the "energetics of bodies" which they seem to like. And I can see that they're getting it. (**Whew!** At least they're not drowning in a pool of dis-ease with their bodies like I was with mine...)

What I was *not* seeing was that I had been passing down – quite unconsciously – all of my collective lies, projections, expectations, conclusions and judgments of what bodies are – should be – could be – can't be – never shall be (dis-eased!) Kind of like a family heirloom: "Hey, kids. Here's a hope chest for you, Christy – a handmade quilt for you, Connor – a family photo album – and a big, old box of crap about bodies."

When our teens started to show signs of dis-ease in their bodies (insomnia, sadness, fatigue, lethargy, anxiety over school, etc.), I dove in head first (energetically resurrecting my former teen "lifeguard" job!) I was determined not to let "body dis-ease" drownings happen to *my* teens. Not on *my* watch. By this time, I was becoming more aware of what I had unconsciously bought about my body when I was a teen – where I was still carrying all of that – and how it may be affecting my kids. Unfortunately, though, we were now all awash in a sea of body dis-ease – and unsure of what it would take to change that.

What questions could you ask?

Fast forward once more. I am training to be a life coach. I learn about the power of questions and I begin asking lots of them. Of myself –

and of my teens. Many of the questions don't have "answers" right away, yet I keep asking anyway. Questions like, "What's right about this that I'm not getting?" (Instead of, "What's wrong with me? My kids? YOU?!") – and "What else is possible here that we haven't yet imagined?" (Instead of, "This is an impossible or awful or hopeless situation" which isn't even a question. It's a statement of judgment.)

The more questions I ask, the more insights come forward. I become highly aware of the role that judgment is playing in all of this. I am also very aware that we are releasing hidden judgments, simply by bringing them up and out of the "secret" realm by asking questions. In a weird way, questions provide a sort of "vocal outlet" for some of those "bottled up" judgmental energies.

I continue asking questions with my clients in my new career as a life coach – and I share my "recipe for living" since I was enjoying "renewed" health (spiritually, mentally, emotionally and somewhat physically):

**1 infinitely-wise energetic being +
1 wonderful body = my great life now**

It was easy for me to see what was going on with my clients – where judgment was locking them up – impacting their bodies – and "sticking" them. Yet it still wasn't easy for me to see all of that completely for myself or my teens.

Time for Action

My body still wasn't all that "wonderful" – I still felt that separation, like I had lost my body in the fog of body projections and judgments that still swirled all around me. Where are you, body? No wonder I couldn't sense it – I had judged it almost completely out of the equation of my life. Every time I bought, told, or sold a body lie – every time I judged *myself* for *anything* (you're not good enough – you're unreliable – you're a failure) – every time I judged *other people* (they shouldn't be doing that – what horrible parents they are) – that fog thickened. I kept to myself, mistakenly thinking that the fog would eventually lift on its own. At the time, that was good enough...

Until it wasn't...

It wasn't like one big, dramatic incident occurred – or the skies opened up – or a huge revelation came in a bolt of lightning. It was more like I noticed that fog creeped over into the kids' lives. They just weren't happy or enjoying life. They were bullied by "friends" who called them "fat" and "weird" – school became a struggle for them – and worst of all, they were physically sick a lot. Everything was hard. Where was that ease that I had started to perceive with my clients? How do we create that for ourselves?

It was time to get back into action for myself and the kids – this time, in high gear with some speed.

Out of the Mouths of Babes

There was another lie that I bought hook, line and sinker. *(Gulp!)* It was the lie that my kids weren't old enough to know what's going on with their bodies – or experienced enough to know what their bodies required (rest, movement, food, water, etc.) or desired (to be with someone, to be alone, to create, to hug someone, etc.) While I had thankfully begun to rekindle my relationship with my body – and was receiving whispers of wisdom from it – I wasn't hearing the part of the wisdom that was shouting, "Hey! Your kids' bodies – like all bodies – have this same wisdom!" Once I acknowledged that, it changed a lot for all of us (especially for me as their Mom). I didn't always have to figure out what was going on with them – decide what to do – make sure that I got it all correct. What I choose to do now is acknowledge and honor what they know – and support them in creating whatever they or their bodies require or desire. Just being this for – and with – them, creates more ease for us all.

I recently asked both Connor and Christy a question related to all of this:

"What effect does releasing judgment have on your body?"

Connor: "By releasing judgment, you're becoming more connected to the source from which you were born (not just your biological mom.) It's that energetic source. Like me, some people believe that it's the Earth that we come from – that our bodies are on loan from there – and they'll return there someday. While you're here on the planet, if you don't judge yourself or others or especially bodies – and if you respect and honor the unique individuals that you and your body are and were made to be – then you will not only help yourself, but you will also help others... their bodies...PLUS the Earth and all the plants and animals on it. Only salmon are created to swim upstream. What are you created to be or do?"

Julie: I then asked Connor to give me an example of what's different now for him, once he stopped judging...

Connor: "I have always been judged as overweight by almost everyone. Once I stopped judging myself in that way – and stopped judging in general – I noticed a few things. I get more energy from my body. I can do more with my body. My body is not as sore after working (at my physical labor job) or playing rugby. I'm more aware of when something needs attention with my body because it's not buried under a blanket of judgment. Something comes up – I acknowledge it – and I choose. It sounds simple. And it is that for me now after practicing being that way. It's very easy to create quick change when I am aware instead of judging, because trying to be both of those at the same time (aware and judging) just doesn't work."

I posed the same question to Christy ("What effect does releasing judgment have on your body?") and here's what she had to say:

Christy: "Releasing judgment gives total freedom to your body for it to create itself. Once you stop judging how it is or how it should be, then it feels no pressure to be anything other than what it truly is. That's the simple magic of releasing judgment."

Julie: A few years ago, both Connor and Christy started to attend some Access Consciousness® classes with me, where we all learned to: (continue to!) ask questions – judge nothing – and create EASE in our bodies and all other areas of our lives. Christy and I also attended Access Consciousness® Right Body for You classes and hosted a radio show called *Teens Done Different* where we talked about *everything* teen-related, including bodies. Several of our shows were called Bod-EASE and we explored various aspects of that, including bodies and judgment. Here's a few words of wisdom from Christy, from those shows:

Christy: "There's a lot of heaviness around bodies. There's a lot of projections out in the world about what to look like – what to buy for your body – what to wear. And I took them all on as mine at one point."

"Your body will do what you ask it to do. If

you say 'I'm sick and tired' of something, the body says, 'OK, we're sick and tired.' There is no judgment of what you say from the body's point of view. It just listens to you and responds to what you say."

"What would it take for all bodies to be viewed and perceived as beautiful? Judgment destroys that beauty. For what reason would we judge something as brilliant and fantastic as a body?"

"Things for me and my body started to change when I chose to stop destroying it. I realized that I'm going to need my body to be up on stage, to give hugs, to smell the rain, to go on hikes and to be with people I like. So, I've got to treat my body like my best friend and be grateful for it."

"When you embrace your own body, you're being an example for others to do the same. You're releasing all the tension and stuck places around bodies for you and for everyone else, when you choose this."

Julie: What is really interesting about Connor's and Christy's responses, is that they both point out how our *personal* choice to release judgment can benefit *everyone* and *everything* around us. What's also interesting is how much "comparison" of bodies we do in our world. All three of us can recall times when we've looked in the mirror and said things like, "Ugh – look at that!" or "That's too flabby! Fat!

Ugly!" and "If this changes, I will not be so nervous around others – I will be liked more – I will finally be accepted" and other insanely judgmental statements.

We've even joked about how it's like our eyes are "lying" to us – or that we've been programmed to be the recruiters for the body image / improvement industry ("Go on a diet! Eating this way will make you physically strong – morally right – socially active! Do this kind of exercise! Buy these trendy clothes and make up!") – and so on...

Since then, we've learned to trust and honor what *we* know. What do you parents (and teens!) know about the effect that releasing judgment could have on *your* bodies?

What can releasing judgment create for you and your bodies?

The three of us continue to release our judgments – untangling them from ourselves, each other, our families and everyone else we are connected to – since we are now fully aware of how pervasive and insidious body judgment and body dis-ease really are. Our invitation? For us *all* to step away from the "comparison reality" with bodies where judgment is normal and common – for us *all* to release judgments that cause dis-ease of all kinds – for us *all* to choose what works for us, thus creating ease in *all* our lives and bodies.

We are often asked how we create our Bod-EASE without judgment. Here's a list of our favorite things:

1. **Stop judging yourself for the past.** Our friend Dr. Dain Heer, co-creator of Access Consciousness® likes to say, "We did the best we could with the tools we had at the time." So, please: cease the judgment of past choices – and choose forward from here!

2. **Ask "Who does this belong to?"** This is one of our most favorite tools from Access Consciousness®. For every thought, feeling or emotion that you have, ask: "Is this mine? Someone else's? Something else's?" Don't look for a cognitive answer. Just notice if something changes or "lightens up" in your body as you ask each question. If it does, chances are it's not yours, so please don't continue to accept that thought, feeling or emotion. Simply say, "Return to Sender with Consciousness attached." (To find out more, sign up for Dain's free video series at www.DrDainHeer.com)

3. **Stop buying – telling – and selling (body) lies**. Now, please! If doing this for yourself isn't motivation enough, do it because the rest of us will reap the benefits!

4. **Ask a question (and dream a little!)** Create an "imagination station" (we have several out in nature!). It's a physical

place (or even a dedicated space of time) for you to relax, dream and ask questions, including this favorite of ours: "What else is possible here (with this situation) that I haven't yet imagined?"

5. **Acknowledge the things that you like about your body.** Dig deep if you need to. Find at least one thing. Do it once a day. Challenge yourself to add another thing to your list every day for at least a week. Having a hard time doing this alone? Get a Body Buddy and be in contact with him or her daily.

6. **Know this (fully and truly):** You can't change other people's body judgments or lies that they project at you or into the world. What you *can* change is how respond to those. Instead of "re-acting" ("re-playing" the judgment or "re-buying" the lies), remember that you are at a choice point when you become aware of them. Choose something other than *reaction.* (How about trying something from our list of favorites?)

We hope that this chapter will contribute to creating Bod-EASE without judgment. Please have FUN while you're doing this. If you do – and your lives and bodies change – please share your story with us at info@JulieOPerkins.com!

JULIE ORESON PERKINS

Since her first trip abroad in 1980 as an exchange student, Julie Oreson Perkins has been engaging in life-changing conversations (in several languages!) with people from all over the world. She continued to develop a global perspective as an International Studies / Spanish graduate from the University of Scranton, PA and an Intelligence Research Analyst at the Department of Defense (DoD).

While at the DoD, she learned the science behind Instructional Systems Design (ISD). Once again, she traveled the globe creating and facilitating professional training programs. She found herself naturally coaching her clients "outside the classroom" on various life topics including relationships (business and personal), job satisfaction, career choices, life purpose and work-life balance.

Hundreds have benefitted from her "conversations of change" as a coach, teacher, motivational speaker, radio show host, energy worker, shamanic practitioner and author. These conversations result in a (re)birth of natural, intuitive abilities and zest for life on the planet here and now. Julie is known for her keen insights, her ability to speak the language of energy, and her capacity to work with clients simultaneously on the Mind, Body and Soul levels.

Julie lives in Boulder, CO with her husband Mark, teens Connor and Christy, and their orange tabby cat Sid. She's someone different: she's happy – healthy and wealthy – a possibilities thinker – passionate about living in a way that works for her – AND she's an invitation to all of that AND MORE for herself, her family, her clients and her communities.

You'll find Julie most at peace out in Nature, where she takes clients to show them different perspectives, possibilities and choices. She also enjoys spending time in the Colorado Mountains, hiking and camping. Always the artist, she loves to create handicrafts like hand-painted silk scarves and scrapbooks with her own photographs.

Visit www.JulieOPerkins.com or email info@ JulieOPerkins.com to find out more about Julie's coaching packages and instructional design services for coaches – or to schedule a session (including complimentary "energetic match" sessions) – or to book her for a speaking engagement. To find out more about her work with teens, visit Teens Done Different on Facebook or iTunes (to listen to podcasts of the Teens Done Different radio shows).

CHAPTER 15

SELF-JUDGMENT, YOU AND YOUR BODY – IS IT SILENTLY AND SLOWLY KILLING YOU?

Kim Malama Lucien

Do you judge yourself? A lot? A little? What about your body? Have you ever stopped to consider how judgment impacts your physical body? Is it possible that judgment, self-inflicted or otherwise, is the main thing that contributes to the gradual decline and the aging process we currently experience? This is big. Take a moment and consider this. Really look at this, be brutally honest with yourself. Do you judge you? Do you judge your body?

For 99.99 percent of people, the answer is a resounding yes. For those of you that aren't sure, I ask you this: Have you ever, once in your life, had that little voice in your head saying something about you or your body that was anything less than 100 percent complimentary? If you can say yes, then you have judged yourself and/or your body.

I had actually deluded myself into thinking that I had slayed the judgment dragon and it wasn't an issue for me anymore! Ha – I was kidding myself. I got rid of some judgment but underneath, it was still there, silently lurking in my subconscious, biding its time to jump back up and bite me! It was running in the background, barely noticeable like a silent killer. Does any of this resonate with you? Even a teeny, tiny bit? I'm going to get into the judgment piece more and how to triumph and kill it once and for all, but first I'm going to take a bit of side trip and talk about our bodies, how they function, communicate and contribute to our lives.

Did you know that your body communicates with you? Everything you 'feel' in your body is actually your body talking to you. Say what?! Some of you might think this total crazy talk! Maybe it is, maybe it isn't. What if it isn't crazy talk? What if your body is constantly talking to you and you just keep carrying on ignoring it?! To add insult to injury, what if you are regularly judging it? Does what we think create a reality in our bodies?

Our bodies are sensate organisms; they are literally a massive sponge of sensations. They are constantly gathering data and information from the people, places and things around us to share with us. They pick up on everything going on around them. Every positive and negative thought, feeling or emotion we have, and other people have, our bodies perceive them. Every judgment we hurl at it, our body hears it, and feels it. Then it starts creating those judgments because it thinks that's what we desire. Our bodies want to contribute to us. They want to make our lives better. They want to give us what we are asking for.

When we only talk to it in judgments, then that is what it thinks we are asking for, and that is what it creates. Most of us do this so many times a day we're not even conscious of it. If we treated our pets, or anything else for that matter, the way we treat our bodies, they would have dumped us long ago. But our body, it's still here, still trying to get through to us with the hope that one day we will wake up and finally get it. Is today the day you get it?

How much more fun could we have? How much more fulfilling will life be if we walked through this life WITH our body instead of constantly being against it? What if the body could be a contribution to creating a life on earth that was MORE rather than less? Is that even possible? It is, it's actually pretty easy. Stopping the cycle of abuse perpetrated with judgment is a great place to start.

Are you sure, absolutely 100 percent certain, that you do not EVER judge you or your body? I was pretty certain that I had gotten almost completely out of self-judgment. Oh how wrong I was. Yes, the really obvious stuff I don't struggle with anymore. I no longer have that constant litany of self- criticism and daily doubt whispering in the back of my mind. I'm now able to acknowledge and appreciate myself and my accomplishments. I thought that meant I was out of self-judgment. As a result I relaxed my vigilance and awareness of where, what, when, and how I was judging me. When we do that and don't undo the judgment the moment we have it, that is where self-judgment gets really insidious, it gets locked in and hidden and starts killing you from the inside.

There are so many kinds of judgment. The ones that really get us are the tiny little judgments that are so innocuous that they don't seem like judgments. This is how it starts to grow, slowly but surely, seeping in like a dark but almost invisible smoke, growing ever larger and taking control in the background, so by the time you realize it, if you do, the darkness has rooted itself into your being and you are living with full-fledged self-judgment again and the judgments are running the show.

Here is a fairytale analogy about light and dark magic (if there was such a thing as light and dark magic, instead of magic just being magic, and how you use it defining the lightness or darkness). Each tiny speck of dark magic you use invites in ever-increasing amounts, and it grows and grows exponentially, until the dark magic takes you over and all the light magic is snuffed out. What is it about this that it's so much easier to invite the dark (self-judgment) than it is to invite the light (no self-judgment)? It's so much harder to get rid of the darkness (judgment) once it is there. This is why vigilance in your awareness of yourself and when you use judgment is so critical; every time a self-judgment goes unchecked, the darkness grows. Demanding total awareness of you in this area is the most efficient path to ensuring it doesn't take over.

So what kind of things am I talking about? I am fat, I am ugly, I'm not smart enough, I'm not talented, etcetera. These are obvious negative self-judgments. We use them to tear ourselves down and keep ourselves small. We know them like an old friend and they are super obvious to us, easy to identify, and be aware of, and change. These are not what I'm talking about. The ones I'm talking about are the sneaky ones you don't realize are judgments, you've misidentified and misapplied that they are something else. Nope – they are judgments.

Another kind of judgment that is not considered a judgment is a positive judgment. How many compliments are actually positive judgments? Positive judgments lock us up and limit us even more than the negative ones. We get to this place where we will only be or do something if we are certain that we will be positively judged for it. What am I talking about? When people tell us things like, you have a beautiful singing voice, or you have amazing hair, or you're so talented with computers. We are so deprived of gratitude and acknowledgement that we cling to these positive judgments like they are a priceless commodity. Then we allow these positive judgments to lock us into place. We stop choosing, or more accurately, will only do or be the things we've decided will get us more positive judgment. Now we will only sing if we've done vocal warm-ups and the accompaniment is perfect. We won't take on that potentially interesting computer project because it might be more difficult than we thought, what if they don't think I'm a computer superstar, what if they find out I'm not really fantastic? This leads to small, limited choices. We start to shut ourselves down more and more and the possibilities in our life and with our bodies get less and less.

We are programmed from the beginning to go directly into the wrongness and judgment of ourselves. To illustrate what the small innocuous judgments could be I'm going to use a personal example, one that occurred very recently and was the genesis for me writing this.

It had been an interesting week and I'd been feeling tired and a bit unmotivated. I was lying in bed still feeling exhausted after eight hours of sleep and not wanting to get up, thinking, oh my god, I've got to get up, I have so much to do, I didn't get this done, I didn't get that done, maybe I'm just secretly lazy, plus a bunch of other similar things running through my mind, all things I should have done but didn't. These thoughts were flowing through my head and as I really woke up it hit me, OMG, I am totally judging myself! I could have been asking my body what was going on. I could have acknowledged that, for whatever reason, this week I need to dial back my 'doing' and that my body required more rest. Instead I was running through a list of what I hadn't done. And then I realized, and this was an even bigger OH MY GOD! All those things running through my mind, that I thought I was just checking into see what's on for today, they are just a list of wrongnesses, all things I was making myself wrong for and therefore judging. I can't believe I didn't even realize that my internal monologue was full of wrongness and judgment. It made me wonder where else I was unknowingly judging me that I wasn't aware of. So I started reviewing my thoughts and internal monologues over the last few weeks and realized I'd been doing it for a while. Yep, I was still judging me and my body.

This is why self-judgment is a slow, silent killer. Most of the time we don't even know it is going on. It's running the show in the background like the little devil sitting on our shoulder whispering in our ear about what we should and should not do. Often telling us that we are nothing, that we are incapable, that we should be smaller and less, and suggesting that we dim the light of our being. This is all happening and we don't even realize it.

Lucky for us we're getting wise to our self-judging ways so we can take actions to change it. And the same tools that get us out of judgment also assist us in communicating with our body! So we are now going to be able to communicate with our body in a way we understand AND we are going to get out of judgment. Changing and improving our communication with our body allows our body to contribute to our life more and more; and getting rid of judgment allows us to communicate with our bodies more clearly. The less judgment the more communication; the more communication the less judgment, and so the circle continues.

It's pretty simple really. Change your point of view, change your life, change your body, change your judgment, changing your judgment changes everything. Our point of view creates our reality; our reality does not create our point of view. When we have a very specific, narrow point of view about something, like what our body is or isn't or how it has to change, then that point of view literally kills and stops other possibilities dead in their tracks. Nothing else can show up. If you stop judging yourself, looking at and treating your body like it is the enemy, a different possibility can show up.

The following tools can be used to end the patterns and cycles of judgment and start changing your perspective and your relationship with your body. Using the tools you will find they quickly become a habit, part of who you be and how you choose. My suggestion – commit to doing them for three days. Why only three days? Because I have ADD and well, most of the other D's, and I never do well when I'm told to do something every day for a long time, let alone forever and I figure I'm not the only one who's like that. Three days is totally doable for anyone. If you forget, do it the next time you remember. There is no right way to do it; there is no wrong way to do it. Play around and figure out what works for you and your body. Approach it like it is a game and see how much fun you can have! I'm certain that after three days the changes, even if subtle, will be worth it and you will continue to practice them until you no longer have to consciously think about them and they become just another part of who you are.

And remember, the Universe works in mysterious ways. Things rarely show up the way we expect them to, so, using these tools might not obviously change something with your body but could instead change something at work, or a dynamic in your family, or something else. Therefore be aware of all the shifts and changes. There is no shift, no change that is too small or insignificant or seemingly unrelated to acknowledge. There might not be an obvious linear connection between you using these new tools and the results that show up.

The simple tools are:

1. Acknowledge your body Every Single Day. Thank it. Have gratitude for

it. Find one thing you like and be grateful for it.

2. Look at yourself in the mirror and say, Thanks Body, thanks for everything you do for me. Do this when you wake up, before bed or whenever you remember.

3. Start talking to your Body. Ask it what it desires. You don't have to do this out loud. (Although I feel the need to confess that I often do!) Start out with the easy things. Start asking your body what it wants to eat, and then listen to what you are aware of.

   • A super easy way to do this is when you are out to eat, run your finger down the menu and it will stop on what your body wants or sometimes I open the menu and I can literally only read one thing clearly. That's what I order. The great thing about this is you can't screw it up. You've been consuming stuff your body doesn't want for years and it's still here, so one more won't kill it!

Ask a question when something is going on, or you are feeling wonky or stuck. Asking a question, really asking, informs the Universe that you are looking for more information. More than the knowledge you have defined in your mind. Asking a question starts to change the flow of energy so something different can show up.

Everything is just an Interesting Point of View (IPOV). When you notice a judgment pop into your awareness, say out loud, or in your head; Interesting point of view I have that point of view. Interesting point of view I have the point of view that my body is_____. Keep saying it over and over again until it lightens up and or goes away.

Pay attention and see what changes you perceive. Acknowledge the changes that show up. Be grateful for them. Write them down – this helps you remember them!

These tools all contribute to easily changing your point of view. Your point of view creates your reality. Your reality does not change your point of view. These tools will facilitate you in doing just that.

If you use the tools, if you are willing to check it out, I'd bet a million dollars something will be different, something will change, even it if is subtle and small. Good luck! Have fun! Make your body your best friend! What else is possible that you've never considered? What will your life be like if your body is your best friend? What will your life be like if you stop judging yourself?

ABOUT THE AUTHOR

KIM MALAMA LUCIEN

Kim has 15+ years experience in the traditional corporate environment having worked with clients from small businesses to large multi-billion, multi-national organizations. She has a Bachelor's degree in Finance, Accounting and International Business from the University of Washington's Foster School of Business. She continues to have a successful career by incorporating her energetic and healing skills with her business knowledge in the corporate workplace. Her ability to read people, to understand others, create good working relationships and effective conflict resolution substantially contributed to her success in that arena. She is a creative genius that revamps your business or your life from the inside out. She has an innate ability to tap into and recognize your natural and unique abilities or strengths and show you how to use them to your advantage. Kim works with management to create systems that are scaleable, malleable and empower everyone in the organization to ask questions, to be decision makers, which directly improves the company and the bottom line.

Her target is to inspire the world, by inspiring the people and businesses that she works with; to inspire through leadership and by invitation and example. To assist clients' movement into a new way of doing business, into a new paradigm of business done differently. The generation and creation of a business based on a sustainable future, sustaining this planet, and being a contribution to its employees, customers and the local communities. To create a future-proof business led from a perspective of awareness instead of 'lack' and I have to get my share of the limited pie, in other words, training companies to be benevolent capitalists.

Kim currently facilitates in a variety of environments from one to one coaching programs, group coaching programs, VIP Day programs. She also has a variety of company and corporate specific trainings to improve and empower your employees and your organization She is also the co-host of a ridiculously fun radio show, Super Scoop of Consciousness on A2zen.fm. http://a2zen.fm/author/super-scoop/, and she is a regular contributor to the A2zen.fm online magazine. Kim also created and hosted the very successful, Aloha Lifestyle Design Telesummit in 2014, www.alohalifestyledesign.com.

You can find her at www.KimMalamaLucien.
com, via email at   kim@kimmalamalucien.
com, or her business Facebook page https://
www.facebook.com/KimMalamaLucien,   Visit her website today to register for her news-
letter, book a session, schedule a training for
your organization or contact her!

CHAPTER 16

WATCH THE "NOT YOU" DISAPPEAR

Janie Smith

When you were a child do you remember your parents asking "Who did this?!!" And you would say "Not me!!" The blame was always on someone or something else. Even if you didn't have siblings did you blame anything on the "Not Me"? My eldest son was an only child until he was 11. We had a miniature Dachshund that seemed to always manage to do these magical impossible things. Like reach things on the top shelves or throw the car keys into the garbage!

I grew up with a sister, me being the youngest. If she said "Not Me" did it, I was automatically the one in trouble. Most of the things I was in trouble for doing, I never did. I was too busy trying to be the "good little girl" and actually scared to death to be "bad". Funny thing was I was always the one with my nose in the corner having yet another think about what it means to be good and do what you are supposed to do! If I said "Not Me" did it, I was still in trouble.

I adopted the point of view that it didn't matter what I did, it was all wrong, and I was all wrong. I started to shut down. I stopped talking. I became a master at internalizing everything. All of this is functioning from judgment and choosing to be at the effect of it. This is a subject I am very passionate about and I'm pretty much on a mission to rid the planet of judgment! I invite you as you read this, to look at the areas of your life where you are judging yourself, going into wrongness, and being at the effect of the life you have created and everyone included. In the same space I invite you to play with the tools I give you here and begin to create your life from awareness and joy. Doesn't that sound like fun? The only thing you have to lose is the "Not Me"! How does it get better than that?

One of my targets in this lifetime is to create our beautiful planet as a judgment-free space to live and enjoy. Ha ha ha! Just a little tiny target! I grew up in a home where judgment came from a biblical point of view. I lived in fear of receiving or projecting any form of judgment and I was always worried about what other people thought of me. Yet there was confusion there as well, because I was being taught not to judge, that's only for God to do, and I was aware that judgment was all around me. Like I could see everyone who was teaching me not to judge, judging everyone, everything, and themselves. I tried my hardest to shut out this awareness and shut off who I was, and to fit into the box that was pre-designed for me.

This created phenomenal physical health issues and the emotional ones as well, like anxiety and depression. You see when you shut off who you are, and try to stuff yourself into a box, it's like putting cut flowers in a vase with no water. How long are they going to thrive? More than likely, not long. I became a master at being "checked out" of my own life.

About three years ago a friend of mine took me to an Access Bars® class. This is one of the core classes of Access Consciousness®. I was determined that this was "just like everything else" and wasn't really going to have any real effect. Boy was I surprised when my whole life began to change! I began that day to get a glimpse of what was possible beyond my decided limitations about what I could choose to create my life as.

I became a Certified Facilitator with Access Consciousness®. I have attended many classes and had the opportunity to travel globally to do so. I facilitate some of the core classes of Access, and using the tools, I have created several of my own.

Through facilitating others and attending classes, I discovered a very interesting thing about judgment. People do not think they have judgments or points of view! How is that possible, I asked myself? With Access we talk about "this reality". What we are referring to is basically everything we were handed when we were born. All the rules and regulations, all the ways that we're supposed to be and not supposed to be, all the ways that we're supposed to create and not create. This reality pretty much excludes all the magic that we know if we chose it, would make our lives fun and easy.

We come into this life with a pre-made box that's built with thoughts, feelings, emotions, beliefs, points of view, limitations and usually lack in there somewhere as well. If this is what we came in with and we never had the knowing that we could step out of the box, what else would we know? So if you aren't aware of where you are functioning from, and you aren't aware that there is a different possibility, how are you going to change that? Well, I would like to create some clarity for you!

Judgment by definition has several meanings.

1. The distance between two points (The original meaning pre-1939 Dictionary)

2. A remarkable punishment; an extraordinary calamity inflicted by God on sinners. (KJV Bible)

3. Determination; decision.

4. Opinion; notion.

All of these are designed to limit. When I function from judgment, I function from thoughts, feelings and emotions. Decisions and Opinions are Points of View. We have been taught that this is a great place to function and be.

We have been taught that life without judgment is not possible. We have been taught that thoughts, feelings, emotions, decisions, opinions, and points of view are significant and therefore real and true. We take all of this significance, solidify it, and proceed to create our reality from this space.

There are so many judgments that are generated and perpetuated on a societal level that we don't even really stop to wonder, is this really true for me? Judgments have been such an ingrained part of living, of what should and shouldn't be real and true, that there becomes a space, if we aren't aware that we can ask questions, it begins to feel like a dark hole we can't seem to get out of. Funny thing is, most of us don't even know we are there! We have bought into the point of view that life is hard and heavy and the idea of having life be any different is some kind of mystical fairy tale that only happens to someone else.

When you are willing to have the space of you with ease and flow, there is no judgment coming at you from you. The judgments coming at you from other people don't stick, and you stop being at the effect of all of it. When you aren't buying into other people's points of view about what you are choosing in your life, what you should be doing, what you shouldn't be doing and all that, you can actually begin to choose what's true for you.

You can actually be present in your life. How

many times do you find yourself functioning from what's true for others and Woops! You find that you are checked out and not present in your life. When you are functioning from other people's projections and judgments, it creates an energy in your world that is like elephants of stuff sitting on your head and it's really, really heavy and dense. Your thoughts might be such that you think you need to fix it.

I would like to share a little about what judgment does.

First off here's an interesting awareness on judgment. It's a continuous ongoing cycle. For every judgment you hold in place, I've been shown that it takes 25 more to hold each one in place. For each of those 25 it takes 25 more judgments to hold each of those in place. It's the ultimate multi-level marketing program of crap! That can feel like an elephant sitting on your head! Not only does it create a heaviness in your world, it's expensive! What?!! Yes, that's correct. Judgments cost you money... lots and lots of money. The founder of Access Consciousness®, Gary Douglas, teaches that for every judgment you buy as real and true, you lose $10,000 per judgment that year. For every judgment you perceive as an interesting point of view, you gain $5000 per judgment that year. Would you like to look at your money flows from that perspective?

Let's look at judgment with money. Would

an infinite being truly have a limitation with money? Of course not! They would create it from somewhere. Money can create a disconnect with people. So if you look at that and see where you have been buying points of view around lack and scarcity then you can begin to clear it and find what's true for you. One of the tools of Access for this is:

"How many points of view about money did you buy from your mother before the age of two?"

So before you could even talk you had all these energetics of what money is, if it's a struggle, if it's easy, or if it's the cause of a bad relationship, or the reason I can't get you things, or money's the reason why I'm stressed out, or money is the reason I don't have any time for you because I have to make money. Can you see the places in your money flows where you have bought judgments, points of views, decisions and conclusions from other people and have created limitations and lack?

This is the reason judgment is expensive. It cuts off all possibilities and awareness. When you are functioning from judgment you can't see beyond the limitations you have created based on your points of view. When you begin to ask yourself...

"Is this really true for me?"

"If I were truly choosing for me, what would I choose?"

This will begin to open doors of possibility for you and you will begin to discover what is true for you. I invite you to notice when you catch yourself judging, concluding, and having fixed points of view, to stop and ask yourself...

"What am I actually creating with this? If I continue with this, what will my life be like in five years?"

Let's look at what judgment does to the body. Every disease (dis-ease) starts with a thought, feeling and emotion. There is a point of creation of a thought that starts a spiral of limitations that creates and can actualize into a physical issue. In this reality we are taught that we create our bodies based on judgment. We can't eat this food because it's not good for your body. You have to exercise a certain amount of time each day to maintain what form you do have. You have to follow a strict diet of bla bla bla to ensure you never end up with a catastrophic health issue, or keep the one you currently have at bay. Judgment is the #1 killer of possibilities and choice on the planet.

What is the first thought that goes through your head when you get up in the morning and look in the mirror? I'm guessing it's something to do with judging all the places that you aren't happy with your body. Like everything that's still there that is less than your point of view as perfection. What kind of choice and possibilities are in that sort of mindset?

Your point of view creates your reality. That which you focus on the most you have made solid, significant, real and true for you. So if a person is focused on the mindset of what's wrong with everything, their body, their health, their money flows, their life, the planet, their job, their relationships... this is slowly killing them and everything else!

I wonder if you were to wake up in the morning and thank your body for being with you again, if you were to tune into what your body is aware of, could you have a different relationship with your body? One that is based on gratitude and awareness, rather than judgment and wrongness? Judgment and gratitude cannot exist in the same space. It's like trying to frown and smile at the same time.

Points of views are basically statements based on judgment that shut all doors of possibility. What this means is as long as you have fixed points of views on things you have solidified them and made them real, true and significant in your world. Points of views also come from the stories you tell yourself and others. What are you saying with your stories? Are you on and on about things like I'm broke and can't pay my bills, or my body is so fat and I can't seem to lose weight, or life is so hard and I can't get anywhere, or I just can't seem to ever win, every time I get close to the top there's somebody there with their hand out taking from me and I'm down at the bottom again.

If your point of view creates your reality, what reality have you created for yourself with your stories, points of views and judgments? The story you tell yourself is basically the life you create. I have a very blunt and awesome tool to use here!

STOP IT!

Stop telling yourself stories that are limited and start exploring possibilities that are unlimited. When you catch yourself saying the old stories that aren't getting you anywhere, you CAN tell yourself to stop it. It will, if nothing else, disrupt the energy and the thought process that was repeating in your head!

Shift Today

Here is some brilliant information, using what I have learned through Access Consciousness® so you can begin to shift this today.

In Access we talk about consciousness, functioning as an infinite being and asking questions. These three tools, along with the clearing statement, are part of the foundation of my other target:

To empower you to know what you know and choose what's true for you.

Consciousness is where everything is exists and nothing is judged. So everything that you are can be. None of it is good, bad, right or wrong, it's just not judge able. What you start to realize with that is judgment is one of the biggest killers there is. It's one of the biggest things that creates limitation for us. When you are functioning from judgment you are always making yourself less than you can be. So with everything being able to exist and nothing is judged it opens up every possibility.

The really fun part is putting this into practice in your everyday life, moving forward from the awareness of that and from the tools that come from looking beyond this reality. Not looking from this reality to try to get further into this reality, but from the awareness that we are infinite beings that have capacities that are far beyond anything we have ever realized.

Asking Questions

Questions open the doors to possibilities. Answers, and conclusions, shut the doors to all possibilities. Here's the key with asking questions. Ask from the space of curiosity and no expectation. If you aren't sure how to be truly curious, watch how children ask questions. They are truly asking from curiosity. Here's another tip, a true question is something you truly don't know the answer to. You can ask a lot of statements and put question marks at the end, however that's going to keep you in the same repeat patterns you currently are functioning from.

Functioning from this reality verses functioning as an infinite being.

In this reality you are taught to judge everything. You are taught that you are supposed to choose something as good in order to choose it, you are taught to choose something as bad so you don't choose that. So you are in this constant search for what's good and only what's good and totally getting rid of everything "bad".

From the universe's point of view, is there any such thing as good or bad, or is it all part of what is? It's the point of view we take about something that creates our limitation about it. If you are saying your point of view in the form of a story, it keeps you in a loop of repeat patterns where nothing is able to change and show up like you would like it to.

With the idea of functioning as an infinite being, here's a tool:

Would an infinite being truly choose this?

If you start to use this with your job, your family, with the places you find yourself not so happy, you will find you have more choices available to you.

For example: you go to a job you don't like, but it gives you the money that you do like. If you aren't doing something you truly love, than you aren't truly living every day when you go to this job. If you do something you truly love than you never work a day in your life.

That's also when the money shows up. Money follows joy!

So here we are thinking that if we have a little bit of money we can create some happiness and some time, that's a "this reality" point of view. Would an infinite being have that point of view? Probably not!

Now it's got to be practical. We can't just go well an infinite being wouldn't choose that. It's got to be pragmatic. If you look at that from a pragmatic place and you go "would an infinite being truly choose the job I'm doing?" No... they would probably choose the amount of money or more and they would also choose to have it show up a different way.

What this means is that you have some other choice available, even if you don't know what that choice is yet, and even if you don't know how to get there. There's some other choice available that's available out there in the universe, you just haven't received the awareness of it yet.

So ok, great, I don't like my job, I love the money, and if I can create it here, doing something I don't like where I feel like I'm selling my soul to the devil... I can probably create even more doing something I love. Now how do I put this into action doing something that I love doing, and making the money, and I love waking up every day?

"If I were truly functioning as the infinite being I truly am, what would I choose?"

It's about creating enough space in your awareness to create both. This is what the tools of Access Consciousness® do. This is about having the space to have it all and be it all. Why not just let go of all the stuff that doesn't serve you anymore and start to bring these tools in? What if you actually had the space to have an easy life?

Another great tool to use when you are asking questions:

Who does this belong to?

98 percent of our thoughts, feelings and emotions don't belong to us. We are brilliant at picking these out of people from anywhere and everywhere and pretending that just because we perceive it in our bodies, it must be ours!

This is where The Magic Wand comes in. Now that you have an awareness of things you would like to clear, you are probably wondering exactly how to do that with ease.

Since you are aware now that you have these judgments and points of view that aren't really yours, you have the choice to keep it or clear it. One of the tools I use is called The Magic Wand. Basically how I use it is "would you like to just let all of this go now?" And "would you be willing to destroy and uncreate all that?" Just by asking, a shift will start to occur. When we are asking if you would like to destroy and uncreate it we are talking about the energetic charge that you have on something making it significant.

So you get the energy of all of the points of view you got from your mother around money, you don't have to be specific about each one and what it was. Then ask "would I be willing to let this go now?" Yes! Throughout all space and time, bring it all up, clear it all out, for now and all eternity. You can discover exactly what this is clearing and what everything means at janielinsmith.com. What I really like about this is that nothing sticks in your world any more. It's like a magic wand that just clears junk with one wave. It also speeds up the process for you to be able to choose something different, be the space of no judgment, and know what's true for you.

I call this my magic wand and use it for everything! When I say it speeds up the clearing process, I'm coming from the place I learned as I was going from Reiki One through Reiki Mastery. This process of pondering, thinking and weighing things was so slow for me. Usually about halfway through the process I would forgot what it was I was clearing, or I would get stuck on something and solidify it even more in my reality. What The Magic Wand has created for me is the space to choose, and the space to be me through choice and question. Now I get an awareness of something sticky and I can ask something like:

"Who does that belong to?

Is it mine?

Is it someone else's?

Is it something else's?"

Cool, return to sender, bring it all up and clear it all out. Then I'm done with it and can move beyond it. How does it get any easier than that?

Science tells us that solid things like walls and houses and things like that are solid because the molecules are moving slowly. What if we have just made our limitations solid and believe them to be real and true? What if they are not actually solid? What if we can just choose to let them go? The Magic Wand goes to the point of creation and the point of destruction and unlocks the things that we had made solid, real, true and significant in our reality. What takes place is we are no longer at the effect of them anymore. It is a tool that is used to create space where before you felt contracted.

Here's the other really cool part! It takes you out of blaming anyone else and yourself for what is going on in your life. You get the choice to clear it and choose something else. See how much lighter that is already? All of this creates a sense of space, and when you have space everything is ok. Nothing really seems to bother you. It's like, I made this choice and it took me down this more limited path and that's ok.

You actually get to start functioning from awareness rather than judgment and then everything around you can change.

The change can only start with in you. You are the one that can begin to choose something different. The only thing you can change is you. There's only one person powerful enough to change you, and that's you! There's only one person powerful enough to stop you, and that's you.

So if you aren't being weighed down by all the elephants sitting on your head, what if you asked...

"What would I like my reality to be? What would I like to choose? What is actually true for me?"

What if you really like bacon and never allowed yourself to eat it because you bought that it was bad for you? Just as an example, but if you look at all the areas of your life where you didn't even entertain certain thoughts because someone said bla bla bla, and you decided and concluded that it was real and true, how many limitations did you create for yourself with that? What could you actually create for yourself if you were to go beyond the confinements of judgment?

If you find that you are repeating patterns ask yourself:

"What's the value of repeating patterns that don't get me anywhere?"

We have never been taught that we are energetic beings. We respond to energetics of things, not so much the words and such. So when you grow up and the energy around things was a certain way, you end up perpetuating that on yourself as you grow up as though that's your reality. Now it may take a while to even be able to realize that there is something out there called "Your Reality" in the mix of things. Once you realize it you start to go "Hey! Wait a minute, if it were up to me I would choose..." and you start to step out of the programming and the repeat patterns you grew up with.

Here's a great question to ask:

"If I had no past and no future to maintain, what would I choose right now, and if I fired everybody that's in my life right now, who would I hire back tomorrow to help me create the life I would like to have?"

Now I would like to talk a bit about nature and the planet. Did you know that judgment is the most toxic thing we project at ourselves and the planet? The planet has so much that it would like to gift us and we continue to destroy it through toxic judgment and choices. This is not something that usually is in our awareness on a daily basis. We wake up in the morning, judge our bodies and what we put in it for breakfast, go to work, do whatever that is all day, come home, do the evening thing and go to bed. Then wake up in the morning and do it all over again. All of it we take for granted, judge the heck out of it, most of that is all done on auto pilot (checked out) and we don't give it a second thought.

How often do you actually go into nature some-where, or go to the beach, or lay in the grass and watch the clouds? When you do take the time to do this do you perceive more space in your world? Would you like to know the reason?!!

The plants and everything you find in nature has no judgment. When you are in that space you are not picking up the judgments of others around you. Have you noticed that? The birds singing in the trees don't go "well you are wearing shoes I don't like so I will only chirp one time for you today". Ha-ha-ha!! Not so much. They love to contribute to you. When you take the time to contribute to the earth you are also contributing to your body. When you create the space where you can have moments and connections of no judgment, you can hear the awareness's the universe has been telling you. Only you couldn't hear them because you had all that racket going on in your head.

In the presence of a shout the whisper goes un-heard. When you are asking for awarenesses from the universe, they often come in the form of a whisper.

What I am inviting you to play with here is what if you could function from awareness rather than from judgment. When you function from awareness you are in the knowing of what's true for you and what's not. You are asking questions and following the energy of lightness rather than creating more heavy elephants sitting on your head. What if you actually create your life as fun and expansive? Would you actually enjoy each day and everything in it as a new adventure?

Have you ever stood outside at night and stared at the moon and wondered How does it get any better than this? It's peaceful and quiet, just you, the night, the stars, and the moon.

Have you ever walked through the woods, stopped and closed your eyes, and took a deep breath of the earthy smell of the ground and the piney smell of the trees and listened to the quiet chatter that is only found there? Reach out and touch a tree, sense its texture and life that it breathes into the universe... providing us with oxygen and life. There's nothing else like that space you perceive there.

Have you ever stood on the beach and stared out across the ripples and the waves that are the ocean? For a moment go there... breathe in the salty briny air, hear the waves echoing across the sand, sense the bubbles of the sea foam popping and fizzing as the water recedes back into the ocean. Aaaaah... breathe in the rhythm for life the ocean provides us.

What if your daily life could be filled with moments such as these? Would you choose it? If you could be in communion with all things, the people, the plants, animals, the universe and beyond. Would that change your life? Would that change your money flows? Would that change your relationships? Would your body be happier? Would you wake up each morning excited for the new day full of possibilities and unseen adventures? Would your judgments and wrongness of you somehow just "disappear"? What would it take? Just C.H.O.I.C.E my friend!
~ Janie Smith

I invite you to play with the tools I have given you in this chapter. I'm not saying that the tools of Access are the end all be all and therefore the only thing that will change things for you. Pick a tool and play with it for a week, maybe something like...

Interesting point of view I have that point of view.

The way to use this tool is every time sticky heavy energy comes up, look at the energy and say "Interesting point of view I have that point of view". Then look at the energy again. Say it again "Interesting Point of view I have that point of view". Look at the energy again. The energy will shift and change. Just keep doing that until it totally dissipates. My challenge for you is to do this for three days straight with every thought, feeling and emotion that pops into your world. I guarantee you that something will change!!

When you have done Interesting Point of View for a few days add another tool. Maybe

Who does this belong to?

Is it mine?

Is it someone else's?

Is it something else's?

Return to sender with consciousness attached.

If you are getting that it's something else's, it's usually a contribution the earth is asking for. In that case you just give it back to the earth. So this is your invitation and your permission slip to play! If you weren't being so serious wouldn't most of your "problems" just disappear anyway? If you would like to expand beyond what I have written in this chapter I invite you to contact me about attending classes that I facilitate! I look forward to meeting you. What if you being you is the gift, the magic, the motion and possibility the world is requiring?

You came into this world as the energy of no judgment. What if you could once again tap into that and become it again? What if you could eliminate the "not you" and choose to be the infinite being you truly be? Hehe! I double dog dare you to be you!

ABOUT THE AUTHOR

JANIE SMITH

Janie is the CEO of Conscious Creations, #1 Bestselling Author in the book I'm Having It, Access Consciousness® Bars Facilitator, Certified Massage Therapist, Seasoned Health and Lifestyle Coach, Entrepreneur, Reiki Master, Creator of Magic, Energy worker, Master Clearer of Entities, Tester of multi-level marketing companies (27 different times with 27 different companies), Mother of 3 boys (18, 7 and 5), World Traveler, a muse for creative inspiration, and a Phenomenal facilitator of inspiring people to step into their potency and create beyond what they could only have imagined in the past.

Janie is the embodiment of "Having It", Change, Growth, Laughter, Fun, and stepping outside of comfort zones. From being the "lone Ranger" in bringing a practice of Access Consciousness® to a town where not many were super interested in changing, growing and expanding, to traveling the world to attend Access classes (Costa Rica, Mexico, Australia, London, Florida), to continuing to expand her life and living even in the face of ridicule and judgment.

"Staying put" is not her forte, Janie grew up in a family of travelers. Her playground was the Oregon coast, Southern California coast, New Mexico, Alaska, Idaho, Nevada, the western slope of Colorado, and currently the Arizona desert in Phoenix. By the time she graduated high school she had been to 17 different schools. With the ocean as her heart song and the mountains as inspiration she continues to create beyond without limitations.

A sought-after facilitator, Janie offers tele-seminars, Google Hangouts, webinars, and workshops worldwide. Her greatest joy comes from creating the space for people choose their greatness and step into their magic and potency. Whether it's her children, people in her classes, her clients, or people she meets in everyday life. Her inspiration and targets are to create awareness in people to know what's true for them, and to be a contribution to expanding consciousness, the planet and everything included in that.

Janie is the creator of:

*9 Elements to Awaken and Include You in Your Life:

Janie facilitates you in creating a Deal and Deliver with yourself, which creates you showing up as you in your life.

*Speaking the Universal Language ~ Talking to the Elementals:

Janie combines the phenomenal energetic capacities the earth has to gift with the potency and magic of bodies.

*C.H.O.I.C.E. To Have It All: Roadmap to Create Your Money Magick
Janie also facilitates the Access Consciousness® body process class: The Bars®

*Fabulous At 40 – I'll have what she's having! Empowering Women To Live Their Best Life NOW!

To schedule a workshop in your area and to reach out to her go to:
janiehealthcoach@gmail.com

You can also reach her at:
www.janielinsmith.com
Facebook:
www.facebook.com/consciouscreations14
Twitter:
twitter.com/janielin147, @janielin147
Periscope:
www.periscope.com/janielin147,
@janielin147
Amazon Author Page:
www.amazon.com/author/janiesmith

CHAPTER 17

WHERE I STARTED TO BECOME
THE AUTHOR OF
MY VERY OWN REALITY!

Ashley McCaughey

What is judgment?!

Do you perceive the energy of this word?

What does it do to your body?

As your reading these words, especially the word judgment, are you thinking of all the "bad" judgments that you have of you or someone else... Now what if I told you that the "good" judgments that you may have of yourself or someone else can stick us WAY more than the "bad" judgments? Let me give you an example.

Let's say a woman has the judgment that she is a sweet darling daughter, such a kind and caring person and makes all her choices in life based on the fact that she is this person, she has two choices... either she agrees and aligns, or resists and reacts. Which actually leaves this person in a no choice universe; she is now defending for her point of view and defending against another's point of view. AAAAAAh! The infinite possibilities that exist in the universe are no longer there, as every judgment is a limitation, if not 10 or 1000.

Now I get that this may be slightly confusing even still, I am going to share a story about something similar that I chose a few moons ago. I worked two jobs back then, full time at the local credit union and then part time waitressing in the local bar on Fridays and Saturdays. I was in a relationship with someone and it actually didn't work for me and hadn't worked for me for MONTHS. The termination of the relationship took this huge weight off of my chest and shoulders, I could finally breathe again. Which was very short-lived as this person began to stalk me in the middle of the night, on my way home from my late night shifts. Interesting creation and choice! Now back to the judgment part of this little walk down memory lane... there were people in my life that actually thought that this person could never do something like that, "he was too good of a guy". Now this is a very extreme example, the people in my life were not using their awareness, specifically. They were using the judgment that this person was "too good of a person to choose that" would have NEVER have been aware of the stalking growing into something else. And it very well could have grown into something else; I was willing to be aware of it. I was very aware that he was choosing that and had chosen it in the past.

In that 10 seconds and for many, many more 10-second increments, I began defending for my point of view, I am right and these other people in my life have NO IDEA and were so WRONG! I was resisting and reacting to their points of view. (Which is all judgment, even me thinking that my point of view was correct.)

As I was working the night shift at the local bar, in the midst of this entire lovely whirlwind I had created, there was someone that started up a conversation with me and ended up giving me his digits. At this time in my life I had not yet discovered the wonderful tools of Access Consciousness®, let's just say that there were no questions being asked back then. I picked up the phone and sent a couple of text messages. I was defending my point of view of the last terrible choice that I had made was so wrong, and judging the fuck out of it. I jumped from one relationship that wasn't a contribution to my life and living, right into another one. WOW it is a good thing that I am cute, that was not my brightest moment.

There were many people in my life that judged me and the person that I had chosen, and I judged myself and this person every day, there was no ease or joy in my life then. So there I was in a relationship that I knew didn't work for me, there were more unkind moments than there were kind moments. I was defending the point of view that I could make it work with this person no matter how much the people in my life defended against my choice. I quit my job and moved a province away from my family and friends to create a life that I knew with every molecule in my body, that the move and the relationship wasn't going to work for me. I couldn't help but cry the first 500 KM's of the trip, one of the many things that I refused to be aware of and my body was screaming at me. Then one day, there I was in the middle of a heated argument, and was pushed. It scared the shit out of me.

I kept saying over and over in my head, "How the HELL did I get here, to this place?" I remember thinking "OK, I created this," which at that point in my life there was SO MUCH judgment of me that I stuck myself with, that for a couple months and choosing something different seemed impossible! Now if I had a few more tools back then, than I could have been in the allowance of what I created and moved on a whole heck of a lot quicker.

Another interesting piece to this puzzle is that I was so bound and determined to make the relationship work. I resisted and reacted to all the points of views swirling around me about how the relationship wasn't working... that I couldn't even see that there were some very abusive things going on. I was defending for my point of view that NO MATTER WHAT this was going to work out the way that I wished it would. The blinders that I had on for this whole relationship were huge, all because I was making "good" judgments of how my life was going to turn out, instead of asking some questions. I was not choosing to be aware.

And let's chat about all of my awareness that I had to cut off to judge my choices and then defend against these points of views and defend for mine! Holy smokes no wonder my body felt heavy 99.9 percent of the time that I chose to stay in that relationship.

Then one day, I knew that if I didn't choose something different that there would be no more of me anywhere, at times suicide seemed like the easiest choice. Shortly after that awareness I made some calls, starting packing and was back creating a life that worked for me and that I knew was possible.

And the craziest part of all the judgment that was in my universe back then is that IT WASN'T EVEN REAL!

Judgment is just someone's interesting point of view, and the judgments that they have of you whether they are "good" or "bad" have absolutely nothing to do with you and so much more to do with the person that is judging you. The "good" judgments are just as much, if not more of a hindrance to you and the people in your life. Those judgments keep you from using your awareness with what that person will actually choose (abusive tendencies in your partner in my case).

I will ask you again, what do you perceive in your body when you are judging you or someone else? Does it make it feel yummy and light and expansive? Or is it the complete opposite... Heavy, contracted, and a not so yummy pile of poo?!

Sharing the tools of Access Consciousness and choosing to BE more and more of me every single day is one of my many targets for 2016. So below are a couple of the Access tools that have shifted and changed my life.

When anything makes you feel light, yummy and expansive it is true for you, and if anything makes you feel HEAVY, contracted and like a pile of poo, it is a LIE.

Let's play with that tool for a moment...

In this reality, you have a body and you drag it around with you. What if you could create something different with your body? What if your body could be this amazing gift? What if your body could share awareness with you to create the life and living that you would like to create, and generate? What would your life be like in five years if you included your body in the creation of your life and living?! When I first actually heard any of the questions above, I was in complete shock. You don't just drag it around with you and demand what it eats and what activities that you take it to do? Mind was BLOWN.

So if you are willing to indulge me for the next 10 minutes, let's play with your body, not like a private moment alone in your bedroom or a private moment with some else tehehehehe. Let's play with your body's awareness.

You are an infinite being and I will share with you a little tool that you can start playing with. Your body will thank you! Can you please put your barriers down and expand your being out to the size of the room you are in, then the building, now the town or city, now the state or the province that you live in, now the country, now the World and now the Universe. Thank you!

1. Pick one thing about your partner, or spouse, or not so significant other that bothers you a little bit or a whole bunch and now judge it even more than you have in the past. It is not significant what it actually is, do you have an awareness of this judgment? Now if you do not have a partner or spouse pick someone that is a contribution to your life maybe a family member, a child or a close friend. How does your body feel?! Does this create the communion that you desire to create in your life with this person or is it creating separation? Is the judgment in your body heavy and contracted?

   When I am judging myself or someone else, I become all contracted and less space, so if you can please lower your barriers even more than the first time that I asked you and expand even more than the time before.

2. Pick one thing about your partner, or spouse, or not so significant other that you are grateful for, fill your whole body up with the gratitude that you have for that one thing. If you do not have a partner or spouse pick someone that is a contribution to your life maybe a family member, a child or a close friend. How does your body feel with it right full of gratitude? Does this create the communion that you desire to create in your life with this person or is it creating separation? Is the gratitude in your body light and expansive?

I'm sure that after that little experiment you have perceived the tremendous difference in your body between judgment and gratitude.

I have attended many Access Consciousness classes over the past three years and I have heard countless times that judgment can NOT prevail when gratitude is present.

What can you choose today to have gratitude for everything in your life? The good, the bad and the ugly! What if you made a commitment to you and every evening before you close your beautiful eyes, you write five things that you are grateful for, in a journal that lights you up? Maybe in bright and colorful markers, or your favorite pen, your journal, whatever it is that lights you up and brings you joy and makes this adventure fun for you! I would choose one that sparkles and the cover is full of pink, purple, blue, red, yellow and green... ummm probably a beautiful unicorn on the cover.

Now some of you may be rolling your eyes at me, you have tried this only to have gotten bored or it seemed to never do the trick of keeping that sneaky judgment at bay from your thoughts and words. I have tried it as well; I grew up watching Oprah every night at five! I have struggled with the "gratitude journal" numerous times in the last 15 years only to cease the process with even more judgment... My god who the hell quits writing things that she has gratitude for? It was just one more thing that I could use against myself in future attempts.

I always knew that there was so much more possible with judgment and so many other things in my life that when over three years ago the phone rang and on the other end of the phone was an invitation to an Access Bars class being hosted by a friend in a nearby town. I asked how much the class cost, the date and what time I was required to be there. I didn't research what it was, what people were talking about on the internet about it, I was going in "blind". I knew there was something different about this Access BARS class than anything I have ever experienced. I have some much gratitude for me choosing that class!

After that BARS class, my life began to change

and shift. Those pity parties that I use to choose or the piles of shit in all kinds of relationships in my life, the piles became smaller and smaller! How does it get any better than that?! And the pity parties that I threw for myself use to last MONTHS and NOW, the pity party only lasts for a couple of days. One of the main factors in the pity parties being for shorter periods of time is that I actually have chosen to have communion with this amazing man that has my back and that will NOT let me play at the pity party for very long.

Now there was sooooo much judgment in my universe before my first Access Bars Class, I wouldn't say that all of it dissipated instantly the minute that I walked out of that little hall west of my home town, gradually it lessened. Like magic, there were choices that I made that I knew weren't the greatest choice for me AND instead of judging me so much that I wouldn't leave my home. There were a set of tools and ACCESS BARS that I could use so the judgment of me wasn't so extreme.

Now I am NOT saying that there aren't times and days that I am judging me or someone else, I would say that it has changed in my world drastically. I can actually have gratitude for me in a world where judgment of you is more valuable. I may not have a "gratitude journal" in these 10 seconds but I can be driving down the highway from work and a whoosh of gratitude rushes over me and there I am listing 20 things that I am grateful for! The sun even if it is behind the clouds, my not so significant other, the truck I drive, my home, my dog, my horse, and on and on and on. That whoosh of gratitude wasn't present in my universe, it was just words and sentences in a journal that would eventually been thrown away.

Another amazing tool that I would like to share with anyone that is searching for something different is "Interesting Point of View". The places in your life that you can use this tool are limitless. One example where this tool can be used when you are judging yourself or you are aware that someone is judging you. Instead of sticking yourself with your point of view or whoever's point of view is being projected at you, if you say as many times as you require, until you perceive the energy shift "interesting point of view, I have this point of view" or "interesting point of view, they have that point of view". You will be pleasantly surprised that the reaction that you use to have to all of the crap going on around you, no longer exists. This delightful tool has assisted me in changing so many insane points of view that I use to have. I have used this tool steady concerning my body, things are changing and shifting. There were times in my life that if my favorite jeans were too tight or one of my shirts didn't fit the way that it used to, there I would be locked up in my home, NOT choosing to do anything because my body was too fat.

Access Bars and the tools that are taught at these Access Consciousness classes have changed my life for the greater. Can we all say together GAME CHANGERS!!! I keep choosing to take these classes and am very fortunate that I have a network of people in my life that keep choosing it as well. In my part of the world we have many BARS trades and last winter we would have them once a week! The change, joy and ease that occurred for most of us were absolutely phenomenal.

Let's do a quick recap of what I have shared with you in this chapter that has worked for me in releasing the judgment in my universe.

What makes you feel yummy, light and expansive is true for you!

What makes you feel heavy, contracted and a pile of crap is a LIE!

You are an infinite being and when you put your barriers down and expand, and start playing with the light and heavy, it will assist you in becoming aware of what is actually true for you.

Judgment can NOT exist when gratitude is present! What can you be grateful for today that would change your whole universe?!?

Find someone in your area that is playing with the Access Consciousness tools and Access BARS! There are Certified and BARS Facilitators all over this planet! Many of them are on Facebook, have websites and are listed on the

Access Consciousness website! They share tools in status updates, free tele-calls, you tube channels and on their websites, so you can start this very second!

Here's to stepping up and releasing the judgment that you have of you and everything in your universe, and blowing all the limitations out of the water so that you can create the life and living that works for you!

Interesting little piece of information, if I would have bought all the judgment in my universe as real and true, I would have never chosen to write this chapter for this book! So where in your life are you buying judgment as true and real that is STOPPING you from being the author of your own reality?!

Who are you today and what grand and glorious adventures can you have?!

About the Author

ASHLEY MCCAUGHEY

Ashley McCaughey was born and raised in Alberta, Canada. In a small rural community where animals and play were in abundance, she was aware at a young age that there was a different possibility with every aspect in her life.

After attending an Access Consciousness BARS class in August of 2012, those possibilities became a reality. She is still attending Access Consciousness classes all over the world. One her many targets is to become an Access Consciousness Certified Facilitator to continue to change the world.

Ashley is a BARS Facilitator and Practitioner as well as an ESSE Horse Practitioner, assisting to create different possibilities with horses and people.

CHAPTER 18

THE JUDGMENT OF SEX

Keisha Clark

It never ceases to amaze me; I notice that every conversation people have, at some point becomes about Sex and/or God. Whether either of those words are spoken aloud or not makes no difference. The energy shows up. That has always been something I noticed and have been so intrigued by. What is it about those words, those energies that the mere hint of them sends most people into short circuit? Despite the fundamental theme in so many of the religious belief structures that *God is Love*, what is more often demonstrated to be the popular point of view has God as the judger and Sex as the thing that requires judgment.

I am fascinated by the endless ways the human race has devised to enforce the judgment of sex. It is so steeped in our stories that most people don't even catch how they have adopted and adapted it into their lives and bodies. Have you ever noticed that? Much of it shows up as cultural practice and belief structures based in the assignment of worth to a body relative to the anatomy it is identified by. I was really surprised to find that one of the earliest applications of the word "sex" was to identify bodies/people as "female" or "male". What jumped out at me about this was that it was a form of separating us from each other. I found that a bit peculiar given that the word "sex" is also used, in modern day, to reference an act of bodies/people joining together. Yes, you could say it simply depends on what context you are using the word, *and* isn't it interesting that in these two cases, one seems to counter the other? Is it any wonder how so much confusion is created around "sex" — is it something we *are* or something we *do*? or both? And does it separate us or bring us together? or both?...

Where There is Beauty

There was a picture in my grandparents' house that I would stare at every time we would visit. It captivated me. I could not *not* look at it. It was a picture of my mother. It was a black and white photo with the slight color highlights. It was displayed amongst other family photos, on a wall in the guest room where we usually slept when we visited. I was so taken by that image of my mother. She was so beautiful to me. The energy of that photo was so alive and vibrant. My mother's smile was dazzling. It was the kind of picture that when you saw it, you just wanted to meet that person. I remember every time I looked at that picture I wanted to be just like her. I wanted to be beautiful.

Some of my earliest memories are of being told by various family members "stop sticking your butt out". Actually, I was never *trying* to stick my butt out. It really seemed to annoy the adults who were saying that to me. It simply did not register for me as a two-year-old, or as a four-year-old. It *did* make me uncomfortable with my body; like there was something wrong with my butt. Was my body broken? Is that what made my butt stick out? Was I deformed? Of course the two-year-old, four-year-old, eight-year-old me did not have the communication skills or the vocabulary to express my questions or have discussion on the topic. And I interpreted the energy behind those commands to mean there actually was something wrong with my butt; wrong with me. This meant of course that I could not therefore be beautiful.

My early childhood and adolescent years were a mixed bag. I don't know that mine was drastically different from what most people have experienced. Each of us has our own challenges. I do remember a number of experiences with kids who were cruel. I did not look like the majority of the kids in school and that drew a lot of attention; not the kind of attention I wanted. There were many afternoons I would get home, go to my room and cry. I would wish so hard for my hair to be straight like everyone else's and for my body to be shaped like the other kids' bodies. I would have given anything to be liked by the kids in my grade school. Thankfully, I was incredibly fortunate to have two relatives who lived close to us, so I got to see them almost every day. When I was with them, I felt beautiful — truly beautiful, the kind that required no demonstration or proof, just beautiful. They celebrated me and adored me. Having them in my life is what made the difference for me; what gave me the strength to choose to not leave the planet before I graduated high school. I'm so grateful for the contribution they were to my life.

So there was a very interesting dichotomy throughout my childhood; an intense unkindness in some people's reaction to me, and the total kindness of a few who adored me. It is really amazing to me that we can experience that kind of thing and grow through it, and live beyond it. I have talked with, and worked with, many people who experienced their versions of this and in every case it is so fascinating. It all seems to stem from the projected value, which seems to be based on what we look like, or don't look like — the perception of Beauty.

The prevailing message threaded through our societies and cultures tells us that beauty and being considered beautiful is what is desired. For many it is what is desired above all else. Another part of that message is that beauty and being considered beautiful will make your life easier. To confuse things a bit, is the variable that beauty is relative - to an endless number of details. Yes "beauty is in the eye of the beholder" and is relative to what the beholder is willing to see. And that is a funny thing about beauty, we want to look at what we find beautiful don't we? This is where it gets interesting to me. I have noticed how people want to look at what is beautiful yet very few of us are willing to truly see what we are looking at, because we are not willing to receive what that sets in motion.

We have many ways we describe our response to beauty — being captivated, mesmerized, spell bound, stunned, taken hostage, knocked out, thrown, or turned on (to list a few). There is another response to beauty that I have observed; fear. Beauty is often associated with power. There are many stories of people being so beautiful, it gave them power over others. In many of the stories the beautiful ones wielded their power (beauty) to manipulate others or take advantage of them. Hence, we have stories of gods and goddesses, as well as many great plays and songs. Those powers usually had something to do with sex — the offer or promise of physical pleasure. Then there is another dynamic that comes into play, the compulsion to possess beauty, to possess that which captivates us.

Some people might say "where there is beauty, there is love" while others might say "where there is beauty, there is danger". I experienced both as I was growing up. I had the experience of being acknowledged as beautiful and being loved. I also had the experience of being acknowledged as beautiful and being treated with unkindness. I came to realize there was fundamental component in all of it — Sex. It took me to the later part of my third decade to begin to cognitively get it, but I finally began to see the energy that was in play through all of those experiences. What I discovered was that energy that is sparked into motion when people see something they perceive to be beautiful, is the energy of sex. What I started to notice was where there was beauty, there was sex. And that created a lot of insanity for people, relative to their learned response to sex, as it has come to be defined in our modern world.

The Power Struggle

What does sex mean to you? Numerous attempts have been made to explain or define sex throughout the millennia and apply various requirements and regulations to it. Sex however, is one of those energies that defies definition. Sex, like beauty, is not something we ever really figure out, or understand. There are so many variables that play into our becoming cognitively aware of sex. No two people experience it the same way. When I am talking about sex, I am referring to an energy that is a great deal more than our anatomy, or a particular behavior, or a specific action such as copulation. The way the energy of sex resonates for me at this point in my life adventure is as the essence of creation; the spark that gives rise to all that is, in our Universe. As I chose into more of my awareness and my knowing around all of this, I became aware of two main ways I had been creating my life. I was either judging sex, or using sex as a judgment. I also came to realize that neither of those methods created anything sustainable.

I showed up in the world as a child with no father. While that doesn't raise as many eyebrows these days, it was quite a scandal at the point in time I made my entrance. When I was around eight years old, one of my day school teachers informed me what a shameful thing that was. In that moment, I totally bought her points of view about what it meant to be the child of an unwed mother. I recognized a similar energy had been present with some of my family members. It had been a kind of secret; it was there — because I was there — but nobody ever talked about it. There was an undercurrent of that shame energy that I had felt but never had anything to mark it with, until that moment. As of that moment, I was something to be ashamed of; the product of wrongness, I was not as good as — and I began to use her judgment against me. My reaction to her judgment of sex was to begin to use sex as judgment. That started me on the course of trying to prove myself as worthy; to prove that I belonged.

I went through all of my teens and well into my adulthood trying to prove myself. I desperately wanted to be beautiful. I wanted to be valued. I wanted to be not wrong. As I look back on it, I see so many places I was choosing insanity by trying to prove that I was valuable. And the really crazy part of it was that I was using sex as judgment *because* I had bought into the judgment of sex! I bought into all the crap about there being a right way and a wrong way to be. I bought the lies of beauty and the lies of what sex was supposed to mean and the lies of what being not like other people was supposed to mean. I gave my power away countless times only to have my judgments of me validated when I would find myself on the receiving end of unkindness. I chose to give up my choice in numerous occasions and situations, putting myself at the effect of people who were choosing total unconsciousness. I kept myself in a constant state of struggle and effort. That is what judgment does. That is what the judgment of sex creates — a diminishment of power that sets up the power struggle, whether it is between two people or within an individual. The thing is, the struggle for power can never be won.

Emancipation

I finally reached the point that it was very clear the only thing my struggle was achieving was my own destruction. The only thing I was proving was that I was really good at struggling. I was very unhappy and my body was breaking down but interestingly, I was still on the planet. I seriously considered dying; it was actually appealing to me at one point. I was aware though that killing my body was not a way out. It would not erase my awareness or my knowing. It would not change anything; I would still be me, just without a body. And judgment would still exist in the world.

I had been struggling for so long, it was like an addiction. Those first months of choosing something different were incredibly challenging. I had shut off so much of me, I hardly recognized who I was. Finally I became willing to look at my life, at what I had created, all the lies I was telling and living; and I began to ask the me I knew I was (and could be) to show up. That was the toughest part, choosing *me*. The part that was most startling to me was how much of my life, how much of me I had been intensely, relentlessly judging. It was massive. I had practically judged myself out of existence. And I realized I had stopped seeing beauty and I had done everything in my power to have no sex, no spark, no creation, no joy. I wept, many times. I grieved. I processed. I screamed. I let my heart break. And I wept. And then...

Something Amazing began to happen — I began to *hear* my body. I had been a practitioner in the healing arts for 20 years at that point. I had also been in theatre and dance through the majority of my life. I was well acquainted with the miracles of bodies. And this was something new and different. This was beyond the marvels of anatomy and physiology, and bodies' abilities with healing. My body was offering me everything she knew — her consciousness, her wisdom, her capacities, her symbiosis and synergy with nature and the planet, and her awareness and communication with other bodies. It was astounding. I had judged my body so harshly, abused her, made her out to be the enemy — and now as I was unraveling the strands of all of that, she was showing me the greatest kindness and offering me the secrets to the Universe. It was like being handed the missing link that joins the unseen with the seen; the unknown with the known. The more willing I was to acknowledge her, the more she could show me. And so it went. I was letting go of the judgments and she was gifting me more of her magic. The shackles I had placed myself in, fell away. And the energy of sex was coming back to life in me.

True Freedom

There is a quote I am reminded of often, from Steve Biko — "The most potent weapon in the hands of the oppressor is the mind of the oppressed."

I have been the master of my own oppression. I have turned my mind against myself so quickly and so often. I have frequently invented reasons to turn myself down and off. I have made an enemy of myself and others. And I have tried to make the very essence of my existence into a wrongness. Happily, I have failed. I am no more a slave to the illusion.

The spark that gives rise to all that is in the universe, cannot be extinguished. We can call it whatever we like. It is potent and it cannot be defined, contained or restrained. We can pretend it does not exist. We can pretend to be afraid of it. We can also choose to Be it. There is power in choosing that. The true power and potency of you — You, Being the energy of creation. Being one with all that is, becoming all you are, receiving everything that creates, requiring no judgment ~ You are truly free.

ABOUT THE AUTHOR

KEISHA CLARK

Keisha Clark is an Entrepreneur, Performing Artist, Speaker, Intuitive Medium and Bodywork Professional, Energy Linguist, and Author with over 25 years of experience in the healing arts and personal development. She is also the creator and host of Living Weal, her international radio show, inviting people to explore the possibilities of Living in, as and from the Willingness to Embody Abundant Living.

Keisha's target in life and in business is to be an invitation to celebrating the different each of us is. Her work is unconventional and shamelessly outside the box, and she greets it with great enthusiasm. As a Living Weal Empowerment Agent, Keisha brings all of her experience, gifts, capacities and tools together to empower people to build consciously co-creative relationships with their bodies, as they are letting go of their judgments of themselves and their bodies; a process she calls *Embracing Embodiment*.

Keisha absolutely delights in facilitating and witnessing her clients and students in allowing more of their true selves to show up. She considers those as golden moments, when we begin to tap into the true wealth of our Being. And she knows when we are willing to make that choice for ourselves, it is a total game changing, life changing, world changing event.

You can find out more about Keisha and the possibilities to work with her, by visiting her website – www.livingweal.com [You might also know Keisha by her long name – Cassondra Clark].

Keisha also co-facilitates healing sessions with an amazing group of cats (yes, you read that correctly) known as The Healing Colony, and you can find out about those possibilities at www.thehealingcolony.org.

And you can tune in to Keisha's radio show – Living Weal – on A2Zen.fm; live on Fridays at 11am Eastern Time, or check out her replays available 24/7 at http://a2zen.fm/author/living-weal/.

CHAPTER 19

BORN FREE

Melanie Meade

I was an optimistic child. I remember thinking what a wonderful world this is. The sun would shine, the rain would fall... a lot, the wind would blow, it would occasionally snow and the world as we knew it would stop and we would play until the snow melted or the sun went down and whatever the weather the world was a magical place to be and that is all that mattered to me.

I began life in the countryside, living next door to my grandparents on a half-acre of land. I remember we used to have a goat, Daisy, who would eat everything in sight. I would feed my Granny's chickens, I would collect their eggs. I would pick all different types of berries she grew for her to make her jam, collect the fallen apples and pick cherries. I would walk through green fields and loved being by the stream, jumping over and back laughing as if we were jumping over rivers and oceans, watching cows and bulls grazing in the sun, orderly lining up in the evening to go back to the farm, climbing up on the old stone walls that must be hundreds of years old covered by trees that separated the fields, where we hid, played and had picnics and sing at the top of our voices. We would go out in the evening as the sun was setting and watch the rabbits run around the field and see if we could find a badger and if we saw foxes we would tell Granny to protect the hens. We dug up potatoes and picked peas and made fortresses with bales of hay and played until sunset. I remember laughing and dancing and running around, playing with kittens and dogs. I saw so much beauty and joy around me.

When I was four, a very simple incident shocked me into realising that not everyone was as happy-go-lucky as me, it was like a mark on my innocence. A young boy in my class one day pinned me up against the door with his toy digger and shoved the pointy edges to my throat and said he was going to kill me. What might appear as a minor boyish incident upset me and I definitely did not what that to happen again. He wasn't the only person to impact me that way. From a young age I lived on alert and decided that in order to stay out of harm's way I was to quieten down that happiness and not share it so much with the world. I was very sensitive to people's reactions.

So I led a secret life of joy, not for everyone to see. With my Granny I could be that unbridled joy. To me she was pure joy. She had the biggest smile that never faded. She was so glam-

277

orous. She always looked well and she loved to sit out in the sunshine. She made a little stage out in the back garden we would Irish dance with her. She made her own dresses and was well known for her knitting. She made our Irish dancing dresses we wore for competitions. Oh we felt so special, there was art work on the front that she lovingly painted on the dress and white lace on the red short jacket with gold buttons. We had an abundance of cardigans, jumpers and mittens. She would make school jumpers for the local schools and my sister and I would sneak up to the door of her knitting-room and peep in the keyhole and watch her measure the children for their jumpers.

I loved her knitting-room. It had a huge knitting machine and we would just watch her work, it was so natural to her. She used always give us silvermints, she kept them in the drawer with her wool. We would try find chores to do for her so she would give us a sweet. She was bursting with love. I just loved being around her. She passed very suddenly when I was seven. She was out dancing and was leaving the dancefloor for a drink to cool down and left this world before her body hit the ground. It was my first experience with death. Maybe even my first real experience with obvious change. The kind of change nobody really likes. It just didn't seem real. I could not understand what had just happened, suddenly she was not around anymore. What was I going to do without her? That woman just brightened up my world. She was my safety net. I am reminded from time to time with the smell of roses from her garden, or if I see sweet williams and willow trees and that unmistakeable smell of wool and silvermints from her knitting-room.

Life was starting to get serious, and I was no longer as carefree and joyful as I once used to be. A big part of my life was missing. This beauty I knew of began to ache, it was becoming impossible for me to be, there was an overwhelming sadness in my heart, it was like I was going into a state of shock, a quiet horror that even a glimmer of being all of me was not going to work very well now that I was on my own. So I grew quieter, sadder and hopeless. I withdrew. I lived in limbo between the mind-numbing smallness of this reality and the ache that haunted me of who I truly was, never ever allowing myself to be. I grew quite suspicious of everything. I lost my memories of what was magical for me. There was no point in hanging onto them and not feeling able to have the freedom only led to disappointment. So I locked them away inside, buried so well that I could not find them even if I wanted to indulge in the fantasy of possibility.

My grandfather was left to live in the house by himself after Granny died. He was a quiet man, loved his space and loved being on his own. He would watch TV and smoke half a Woodbine and save the other half for later because he said it was better for his health.

He used to be a Sergeant in the army and went on peacekeeping missions for the UN. He was a broad man, relatively tall, to me a giant. He was a strong man with a deep firm voice and was a product of his environment. I loved my grandfather but he was mysteriously different.

A stage came where we would almost every evening be in the front room with my grandfather, my mother and her only sister, and we would all be saying the rosary. It would happen a lot. I always knew there was something strange about it all. This was around the time he was diagnosed with cancer. It was very much kept from us until just before he was admitted to hospital as we were quiet young. I saw none of it, we had no idea and we lived next door. He had a wheelchair, I never saw it. I do remember a walking stick but with his limp he always had, I didn't think too much of it. He was a stubborn man, he resisted help and would crawl through the house from his front room to his bedroom. He would not give up his independence. He fought right until the end. This man never stood down.

I knew when the day came he was to die, we were kept home from school and there was a storm. I remember the wind and rain and I remember the phone call. I knew when that phone was going to ring. Dad was home with me and my brother and sister and my mom was in with her father. They sat with him and said the rosary and on the last prayer "Glory be to the Father, the Son and to the Holy Spirit as it was in the beginning is now and ever shall be a world without end, Amen." He finally let go of his rosary beads and this life.

My life went on. I had lost my bright and bubbly grandmother and the mysterious force that was my grandfather. It was like I was growing up fast in this world and that magical beautiful childhood I once had was disappearing even more. There was so much sadness in what I saw as a beautiful world. It just made no sense to me. I was so confused. Just like my granddad, I became more of a loner, distant and I used to get very frustrated. In order to control that wrongness I fell into a kind of military behaviour of form, structure and control. I used to be called the Sergeant Major and the Ice Queen, I was organised, I had no time for nonsense, I would get the job done and keep the peace, just like my grandfather and I nearly walked like a march and I could bark like a Sergeant Major too. It was like a way of shutting my way of being me out and falling into a discipline that was so linear, militant and functional – I was just about surviving in this reality. I felt I was safer to be this way.

I felt so wrong. My confidence was low, I felt worthless. I saw how my grandfather used to withdraw, he needed his space, he was stubborn and would fight on regardless, and I identified with that. I took on the judgment of how wrong he was for all his shortcomings and bought it as mine and ended up resenting my grandfather for ending up like him. I had become so withdrawn I became passive and even more introverted in an effort to be less like him and I no longer let my frustrations out, I actually bottled everything up inside and locked myself away from the world. This left the door open for years of torment from some very unhappy and angry people. It was almost like I deserved it. The torment matched the pain inside me.

Many years had passed and one day it all changed. I remembered over the years seeing pictures of my grandfather in Cyprus or the Congo and other places he travelled as a peacekeeper. He was a strong looking man, with a very strong presence. He was a force to be reckoned with. I also saw gifts he brought back his little girls and how they were never too far from his mind either. He did have a soft side, a gentle side. I can remember a family recording of him coming into my kitchen with open arms to greet my sister by the door, picked her up and squeezed her. He had a smile on his face and a hearty laugh, he was capable of love and happiness too. I had forgotten all of that. I locked myself up in what was wrong with both of us.

There was no fear in my Grandfather other than the fear of being his true self. A story I was told about him epitomises him to me a moment in life where he truly showed up. He was on a peace-keeping mission in the Congo. My grandfather and his men were out in the jungle and the local tribe, who were highly skilled, brutal warriors and cannibals, were drawing close. They all hid in the jungle all night trying not to be detected, for if you were found, you would meet a brutal and bloody end. They were found eventually. The leader of the entire tribe was notoriously ruthless, he was known for no mercy. My grandfather and his men had the misfortune of having the tribe leader present when they were found. So facing a violent death my grandfather stepped forward and came face to face with this merciless man. They stood toe to toe and he looked the leader dead in the eye. What did he have to lose? No words were spoken between them both as they faced each other down and then all of a sudden they were all free to go and they peacefully just walked away. My grandfather stood up to the most merciless man with just his sheer intensity, he was not going to just stand by and allow everyone, including him, be slaughtered.

It spoke a truth to me and it took a long time to actually acknowledge the capacities of this man, it explained a lot of what people thought was odd with him. One day I just looked at it all and it turns out we were not far from different to each other but not because we were cold and distant but because we saw everything exactly as it was and we had a way about us that was a kindness where we could go toe to toe and face to face and say not today, we knew there was another way. Not everyone appreciates that fierceness and we did not really know what to do with it but just step back, shut down and feel wrong.

He was as misunderstood as I was. He might have dealt with his frustrations in ways he would have preferred not to, he did not know another way at that time. I now get the gift that there is another way of being with that same kind of awareness and intensity and not having to go to that place of shutting it off like he did. It was a truly amazing quality he had that he never appreciated himself. I am grateful for him showing me this.

When everything started to fall into place for me and things were going to change I was in my 30's. A now single mother to a beautiful, bright, smart, fun loving, little go getter. From the moment he was born all I desired for him was to live free from limitation, to be a leader in his own life and for him to know he was more than enough and never too much. He gave me a glimmer of hope that beauty still existed in the world, he made me smile again, he melted my heart and softened the harshness I felt around me. All I wanted for my son I had forgotten was still available to me.

When I finally included me in my desires, I finally acknowledged that I had a strength, a way, a tenacity and intensity that was not wrong and it was like a light switch had gone off! So I just started living. I stopped holding my breath, I began to inhale and exhale and open my eyes to the beauty that I once knew surrounded me, it hadn't gone away. Gratitude increased in my world for me. I was becoming more aware that it was "I" who got to create my reality, not anybody else, that I was FREE. The loneliness that had once existed in my world was that I was missing ME.

That is when I had set myself free and started to remember me and all the magic and wonder I knew existed. I saw everything exactly as it was I even saw the beauty in things this world did not see as beautiful. It was only when I bought society's points of view as real I saw things as right and wrong. My Grandfather and I shared a dismay at the world we lived in and the desire for peace, knowing something greater was available. That intensity we both suppressed, when set free, is even more intimidating to people – it is so real and so raw almost unseen in this reality. I no longer fear exploring it as I now realise this is a strength not a wrongness. It can still prove a bit tricky for me at times but that's okay too. I am choosing towards more of me and the freedom to be and sometimes that requires a little navigation.

It became more about not how was I going to deal with the world, but how was the world going to deal with me! If there is nothing wrong with you and nothing to fix, what would you choose? I chose play, exploration and the adventure of living. What if being free was that quiet contentment and gratitude for you just as you are, right now, in this moment – free from fixing and searching for solutions to find this happy life somewhere else out there in the world. What if what you have been waiting for was you?

When did you judge yourself out of existence, out of the greatness, uniqueness and exuberant living you were born with? Ultimately, what did you make bigger than you that made being free to be you seem impossible?

Judgment is our jailer. Judgment is not what other people say, do or think about us, they become judgments and can only stick if we believe them. Only you can imprison yourself and only you can set you free.

I had lived that wonder and magic and I had lived in my own judgment. Trying to squeeze into the "shoulds" of this reality did not give me the peace I thought it might, that low key under the radar, don't stand out kind of peace we think exists if we don't draw attention to ourselves. In a world where being you was determined by your job, social status and so on I genuinely thought I was wrong and there were rules to follow on how to be yourself I truly could not master. I lived in constant judgment of who I was, how I did things and a confusing inner battle ensued as I supressed who I truly was.

The question is not who judges you or what for. The question to ask is what have you judged you "as" or "as not" that will not allow you to be that uniqueness this world secretly craves? Are you ready to surrender your way of functioning in this world that is your survival mechanism for existence and instead choose to set yourself free and soar?

We twist and turn events to make what we think true and solid, to keep us "safe" and justify as to why we "can't" and negate all that we know and deprive this world of greater possibilities.

I had the world at my feet as a child and when I started feeling all wrong about how amazing I was because it was different, I mimicked a man that didn't know how to be his intensity in this world either and I ended up resenting him for being who he was – it was more likely I was resenting myself for not allowing myself to BE. We shared the same tenacity, the same potency, the same clarity and also the same helplessness with not knowing what to do with it in a world that found our ways quiet challenging.

Is now the time to break the rules of this reality and be you, all of you, without apology? To permit yourself to be that beauty, that presence, that contribution that creates a better world beyond imagination. We are far more than we think we are, thinking can only take us to a point in which we have some kind of familiarity of our upper most limits of awesomeness. What's beyond that? Are you ready to lose everyone else's points of view of what you can and cannot be and inspire the world to greatness? The only person stopping you is you.

Imagine a world where judgment ceased to exist... even if it was just in your own world, what would you create? For me it's an ease where everything is a possibility. I have defied a lot of the limitations imposed on me growing up. I have broken a lot of the rules of this reality. I gave up the fight, the resistance and I surrendered to my own desires, my own reality and my own greatness. Consciousness is a journey not a state achieved – it's a whole new world of uncharted territory, it's an adventure. What amazing possibilities are a choice away? You are free to choose! I choose me.

ABOUT THE AUTHOR

MELANIE MEADE

Melanie Meade has a desire to create a world where judgment does not exist. Where your superpowers can come out 24/7, not just when you are home alone. Melanie invites you to a life where you have the simplicity and gentleness that change can be. Where the ease of creating is second-nature and where you get to be the magic of you, whether anyone sees it or not. What if your life could be bigger than you've ever imagined?

What can Melanie contribute to you? Find out more at www.melaniemeade.com.

CHAPTER 20

IF IT'S NOT FUN, COULD YOU FIX IT?

Susan Shatzer

One of the most interesting phenomena of judgment for me has been the way it NEVER works with my son. Over the span of 13 years, I have often been required to seriously examine how I was showing up and what that was creating. Nicholas used to and in fact, still does most things not at all the way I think they should be done, ought to be done, must be done or have to be done. I laugh as I type this because I can picture many different events where I was sure I was absolutely, positively right and was forced to take a step back and deliberately look at what I was literally asking, at times, even demanding of him. I've been lucky enough to have received powerful awarenesses, more like kicks in the butt, which could not be disregarded or pushed to the side and addressed at a later time. What if my child may actually be here to teach me something and not the other way around? What if my judgment of him and the way he was acting generated what was required to create the change necessary to facilitate more ease and ultimately more fun in our lives?

It just so happens I grew up with amazing parents who are still married and count my blessings for having one parent that was extremely laid back and one that was a little bit OCD with a heaping side of controlling mixed in. I love them both equally and have had multiple conversations over the years with them as to their parenting styles. One was not right or better than the other. They were both completely different and I'm glad I had the combination. My son on the other hand has divorced parents. One parent full time, and visits with the other on occasion. It has been the greatest gift for both of us to have separate living locations. It has allowed each parent to manifest their own parenting style without constant judgment from the other about what he or she might be doing wrong.

At the time I became a parent, I noticed just how much I embraced and projected both parenting styles toward my son. I would be manic in one direction or the other. Nicholas seemed to do better and reacted with greater ease when I was laid back, and he was more in the driver's seat. I even noticed that when I asked him questions about what will work for him instead of demanding what will work for me, the suggestions he made ended up working for both of us. His choices had me evaluating on many occasions my stance on: "We have to do this. You have got to do that," philosophy.

I would carry the importance of this mindset with me as long as I could and fight for the rightness of it, using body language, facial expressions, sound effects and carefully chosen words to judge him into doing what I wanted him to do.

Surprisingly, it didn't work, and much to my surprise, wore me out in the process of defending my point of view over and over again, never actually winning the battle. I had to step back repeatedly and re-ask myself, "Do we really have to do this now? Or, does this have to get done today and this way?" Close to every time, definitely more often than not, we did not absolutely have to do anything. And in not demanding the completion of whatever the task I had originally marked as "HAVE TO", it showed up at a completely different time and not at all how I thought it was going to which ended up, I have to admit, actually being way more FUN. I held onto for dear life, the correctness of I'm the mom, the adult and I know what is right and the best in all situations about everything. Can you relate to this? Well, I'm happy to say, that is so very much NOT true. I have, through multiple failed attempts to be RIGHT and CORRECT, realized I am often not.

As soon as I was able to release the power of judgment, I simultaneously acknowledged he actually might know what works best for him. I was then able to get out of not only his way but mine as well. I tried to stop micromanaging and helicopter mommy-ing him but allowed him to have greater choice when possible. No matter how young, small, inexperienced, un-educated, and so not his job the family, society and my thoughts had of him, I still attempted to include him in the decisions. It worked and I saw more and more ease show up for us. I began choosing to modify my parenting style and take on a different role when possible. It was not only one of co-creating our lives together but also one of the greatest gifts which would contribute to both of us being who we are and doing what we love the most and are really good at.

Nicholas constantly out-creates me and I love it. When he was little, and having a meltdown, I would ask... "How long do you want to be sad?" And when he would answer "ALL DAY, MOM" I didn't try and make him wrong or fix him. I reframed from judging him with words and ac-tions of "Grow Up." "This has to stop." "You're too old for this." What I did do secretly was provide examples at a later time of how quick-ly I could choose something different. When he saw me get upset, I asked him to keep track of how long it took me to change. After a few times of demonstrating, he got it. We now can have a knock down drag out scream fest and within 30 minutes, we are both on to choos-ing something different. It is amazing to see how fast he can shift and move on from dis-appointments. He doesn't tend to carry them around like baggage looking for validation of how bad he is, but checks them in, lets them go, and forgets about it. He is exceptional with releasing the thoughts, feelings or emotions attached to judgments and not storing them for future use. I on the other hand fall back into old patterns by asking "Are you really OK with this?" and "Are you sure it isn't bothering you?" Interestingly enough, I often catch myself searching for the polarity and judgment he should have but doesn't. How brilliant is he? I'm still learning.

Together we have journeyed through pre-school, Kindergarten, elementary and now the conclusion of middle school. By releasing the judgments I had as a parent, life showed up in the way I never would have thought possible. I was, after all, a certified requested elementary school teacher and was convinced homework had to be done in a very quiet area, have exceptionally good lighting, require a sharp #2 pencil, work to be completed in its entirety on a flat surface with absolutely no fooling around because "Learning and Studying Were Very Important". I literally became the homework monitor and was on patrol the moment he entered Kindergarten. As he grew up, I couldn't stand how he wanted to lie on the couch or sit in a recliner to complete his homework. I remember having so much trouble and fighting with him over finishing every bit of homework while listening to music in the background. Until one day, as if a bomb had gone off in my world, I happened to be sitting on the couch next to him while he had his school book open, the TV on and his father called. I witnessed him talk to his father on the phone, read from his history book, and listen to the TV. I sat there and stared as he continued with his conversation, watching the show and jotting things in his book all at the same time. I couldn't believe it. He was processing three different channels of information all at the same time. After I quizzed him for undeniable proof about all three, I realized he was successful at all of them. Can you believe it? I was stunned and more importantly, it was the day I gave up my self-appointed job of Homework Monitor. He now completes his homework on the computer while watching YouTube videos on his tablet and listening to music. He is in the highest level of public education while earning high school credit in middle school on top of consistently achieving the honor roll. Who knew I could be that wrong and my child would actually know what worked for him? Shame on me, right?!

I carried that wrongness around like a good mother for a very long time which did neither of us any good until I realized, I could choose to let it go. I asked myself, what benefit is it to ferry the judgment of being terrible, mean, awful, bad and completely wrong; which I was after all; with me all the time? Once I released the power which judgment had on me, there grew more ease for the two of us. It gave me the energy and time to choose for me which was up until that point dedicated to my suffering in the wrongness of me. It allowed the two of us to enter into a conversation that moved in both directions.

I have to admit, that was the day I definitely, intentionally, and purposely gave up everything I thought I knew was real, right and completely relevant with parenting. Today, Nicholas and I ask a ton more questions about what works and what doesn't work for both of us. He is now part of the equation. We ask questions to give us the clues on what is the best for us. We'll ask things such as; What can get done today? Which things require more time? What can you do and would like to do? What can I do and would like to do? What can you do by yourself? What would you like help with now? It has been interesting to watch the abounding and incredibly different possibilities that have shown up. Nicholas cooks plus does his own laundry and dishes. He takes care of the trash, lawn, pool and six reptiles. He grocery shops, including assessing the size, price and content of items as well as successfully picking produce, ordering from the deli and distinguishing what to look for when choosing meats.

We laugh together more and more each day. Periodically we will ask each other "Are you having fun yet?" And if either of us says NO, we immediately respond with "Then Let's Fix It!" A couple Christmases ago, the extended family was coming to our house from out of town and to save space, they shipped Nicholas' presents to our house ahead of time. It was thought-provoking how all of a sudden numerous packages commenced arriving. Multiple times, I wasn't home to collect them before Nick arrived from school. He would not only see these boxes and bags but carry them in. It just so happens, that specific year there was an extended amount of vacation time prior to Christmas Day. He was relentless on a daily basis about asking to open the boxes, knowing full well, they were his presents. He is a creator of magnitude and discovered what it was going to take to get me to agree to let him open his presents. He asked, "Are we having fun yet?" and when we both answered with a resounding "NO!" I thought, Why the Hell Not? What is the benefit of making him wait until everyone is present to open his gifts when we could be playing with them right now? So began the pre-Christmas present party with a monumental amount of joyous enthusiasm. He opened every single box, read the directions, put together the pieces and played with everything over the course of four or five days leading up to the family's arrival. This choice totally worked for me because I was parenting 24/7 solo with a youngster. Until, one day, I stopped in my tracks and had the awareness, Nicholas would have to show a convincingly surprised look on his face at the time he opened these gifts in front of the family. So we practiced, and laughed, and practiced some more. It was the funniest thing we still talk about today. Together we stood in front of each other and other times in front of a mirror to practice our facial expressions, our body language, our voice inflections, and to our delight, no one was the wiser. Not a single family member figured it out. How wrong would I have been to have not only allowed my son to open his presents but to play with them too? A trillion times a trillion for sure. That was one of the very best Christmases ever. I admittedly have shared my criminal activity since that time with those family members inflicted by my reckless decision-making and they received the news relatively well which was extremely surprising to me. How can it get even better than that?

I have found from personal experience, releasing judgment of both myself and my son, Nicholas, was one of the greatest gifts I could have given the both of us. It truly doesn't matter what worked for my parents or what the rest of the family thinks, or even how our friends are parenting but being true to what actually works for us is the contribution to each other in our lives. Literally my entire parenting style was thrown out the window and has since shifted to co-creating together. It takes the burden off of having to have all the answers and being right, good, perfect, and correct all the time. The minute I was willing to release judgment and step into a different parenting style possibility, it felt as though millions of shackles from lifetimes of collective, cultural, familial and feminine bondages were released. I now look for and ask, "What else can we do, be, have and create together today that will be way more fun than yesterday?" What if you tried something like this and it worked?

ABOUT THE AUTHOR

SUSAN SHATZER

Susan Shatzer is an International Consciousness Revolutionary and a three-times #1 Best Selling Author of:

- *I'm Having It*
- *The Energy of Spirit*
- *Creations: Conscious Fertility and Conception, Pregnancy and Birth*

She is a seasoned TV and Radio personality having been on the Lifestyle channel, MNN Network, LA16, and most recently on the "Ask-BonBon" TV show. Susan's run a successful coaching business, became a Bars, Body, and Certified International Facilitator with Access Consciousness® and now, as the CEO of *From Creation to Cradle*™, she incorporates what she has learned through many diverse experiences to create programs that empower women before, during, and after pregnancy around the world. Creator of *Conscious Birth-*

ing and Beyond and the author of the book "108 Ways to make Money Fast", Susan's hope is to empower individuals to leverage opportunities and avoid despair when facing financial difficulties because no money seems to be there.

A Selection of Susan's Workshops and Events include:

- What If Getting Pregnant, Being Pregnant, and Giving Birth was Joyful?

- Roll-Up Your Judgment and Undress Yourself with Kindness!

- Having Money, Wealth and Abundance in Any Economy!

- What if money REALLY *wasn't* the problem, YOU ARE?

- 52 Body Processes to Change Your Body and Your Life!

- How to Become Money Now and in the Future?

- Ask A Question and Change Your Life on Purpose!

- What if we are the change the Earth requires?

- Magic! You are it! Be it with your Business!

- Stand and Command a Different Reality!

- Relationships and Parenting Made Easy!

CHAPTER 21

THE CATALYST OF ALLOWANCE

Betsy McLoughlin

"You are so accepting and in allowance. You are the space of no judgment." I am hearing these words from friends and clients and as I truly look at these words, I am so grateful to be that space and invitation. And I marvel at how this happened.

To me, allowance is a gift of kindness and honor. When we allow others to have their points of view without criticism or judgment, it truly honors them. There is no good or bad, right or wrong. Allowance creates the space for people to choose for them. It is a nurturing energy to be received in total allowance. When you have a conversation with someone that is so easy, that's the space of acceptance and allowance. Allowance is the catalyst for much change.

I grew up in a judgmental home. Bigotry and discrimination of every possibility were popular sport for my parents. My father was a walking bundle of judgment. My mother judged her body, everybody else's body, what people wore or didn't wear. She judged where people lived, the cars they drove, where they shopped, and so on. She criticized my body relentlessly. I don't know any area where she wasn't a walking, talking judgment machine.

I felt like I could never please my mother. No matter what I did or said, she judged and critiqued me. I also felt like a big pile of useless poo much of the time. In the space of her judgments, I concluded that I was never good enough, pretty enough, skinny enough, or smart enough. You get the picture! This set me on the path of choosing victimhood and feeling sorry for myself for a long time. I accepted the constricting point of view that I would never measure up to my mother's impossible standards. I didn't know anything about allowance for myself, for her points of view or anyone else.

Our society is steeped in judgment. We are bombarded on TV and movies about whatever the perfect body is for that year. There are shows where all the hosts critique outfits worn by celebrities. They seem to take great pleasure in criticizing what someone wore at an awards show. Paparazzi camp outside celebrity homes and if they snap someone without makeup or perfect hair, that image is strewn across print and social media with tons of comments along the way. Judgment is everywhere and it is insidious.

When I was in high school, I was very aware of my father's bigotry and it made me feel extremely uncomfortable. I resisted and fought against it. It didn't make sense to me that you would immediately dislike someone if they looked different from you. His opinionated points of view extended to those that didn't align with his and he said degrading things.

I chose a different path from bigotry. I swore I would be different from my father. I did not participate in the limiting points of view of seeing skin color and not getting to know the person behind the skin, body size or anything else.

I didn't see judgment for the constraint it is. Judgment seeped insidiously from other aspects and I was an active contributor. I slipped into autopilot of being a judgmental adult. I constantly judged myself and everyone around me. I participated in everyone's gossip and critiquing of each other. I was very aware of all the criticisms swirling around me. I accepted all these judgments as truth and piled them on top of my own. It got to the point where these judgments weighed me down like a dense, heavy fog I couldn't see past. I built a fortress around me of criticism, condemnation and heaviness.

I fell in line with women complaining about their husbands non-stop. It hit me one day how much I did this unconsciously when my son said something critical about his father.

He was around seven or eight years old. He was repeating something I had said several times. This was one of the factors in me choosing something different. I did not desire for my son to grow up resenting his father as I had chosen to do. It hurt me so much to hear my son parroting what I had said in anger and passive aggressive mode. I gently sat down with him and explained how unkind this comment was. I told him I was no longer going to speak about daddy that way. I asked him to please only speak kindly about his father and told him I was sorry. He looked at me with his wide-eyed innocence and took it all in. He gave me a big hug and told me it was ok.

I felt terrible that this was the example I was setting for him and it was a huge kick in the pants for me. My son shone the light on what I was choosing to teach him unconsciously. I realized this also gave him permission to speak about anyone else in that tone – including him! That was not ok with me in any way. I am so lucky to have such an amazing son. As I changed my behavior, my relationship with my husband changed for the better in every way. My son is now a remarkable man who is kind, generous and accepting.

I was unhappy and ungrateful about most everything in my life. I complained about everything and anyone. I realized that it was not generative for me to live in this space and I made a conscious decision to change this habit and way of being. I functioned from the space of the glass is half empty mentality. I began to wonder how I would choose to live the same life that my parents had chosen. Didn't I desire more?

In taking a hard look at my behavior towards my husband, I saw the example I was setting of disrespect and dishonoring. I am grateful for the harsh mirror I saw with my son mimicking my behavior. I saw how unhappy I was in that environment. Feeding the passive aggressive, petty, judgmental, bottomless pit monster was destroying my health, my marriage and me. And I sure as hell was not going to teach my son these behaviors any longer.

It was at that moment where I clearly saw I desired respect, honor and gratitude in my marriage. I was so pissed off that I wasn't receiving that from my husband without looking at where I contributed to the lack, distance and separation going on. It sure was easier to look at what he was doing instead of looking at my behavior that might have contributed to the situation and the endless cycle I was trapped in.

The energy of judging, criticizing, passive aggressive attitude and unhappiness had taken its toll on my life in a myriad of ways. I said enough of this — time to STOP this destructive behavior. I no longer desired to live like this. I realized how much time I wasted being in this small space of judging.

As time moved forward, my automatic pilot of judging diminished greatly. When I heard myself judge, I stopped. I was uncomfortable being around those that judged and complained. I didn't even want to be around anyone who did that and would avoid those people. My son and I no longer said anything dismissive or disrespectful about my husband or others.

As I demanded respect of myself for the first time, people began treating me with the very thing I had desired for so long. I had wished and demanded respect without having a clue how to get it or give it. I was not taught respect growing up and I had the power to change that. I did not have to continue blaming my parents for what they were doing and how my life turned out. I taught myself self-respect. I chose to honor and appreciate myself for the first time. It is healing and generative to live in this space. Who knew? I wonder how the world would be if we all chose to be like this? I'm sensing pretty friggin' awesome.

Many of my friends stopped coming around when I did not participate in the complaining game. I found it fascinating that they did not desire to choose beyond complaining.

Have you ever stopped and really noticed how many people complain about everything? Have you noticed how much judgment and criticism is all around us? If it's cold or a rainy day or the sun is hot, we hear someone griping about it. What about when the snow is falling? We hear wives complaining about all the things their husbands don't do and husbands complaining about their wives. Comedians make a living joking about all the complaints! Oh my gosh, it can be overwhelming.

Unless we have the ability to be on a desert island alone, we will hear judgments from others. So, what do we do about it? Normally when you are being judged, you automatically put up barriers and do your best to block the judgments. The trouble is that we don't really block them. We go into defensive mode. We spend time deflecting and defending. When we dress in the morning, we put on the heavy armor of defense. Each day the armor gets a bit heavier. The judgments attach to us. And over time, they pile so high we can't move.

When you are in defensive mode, the automatic barriers go up. When the barriers go up and you're in that state of deflection, how much are you able to receive? How much love, joy and happiness are you deflecting because you are too busy with your shields up fighting off the perceived attack? It's like the Star Trek movie when the Enterprise ship is going to be attacked and you hear the captain order the shields up for defensive maneuvers. How many hits have you taken even with your shields up?

What if refusing to receive judgment is only necessary if you believe judgment is real? What if none of it was significant in your life?

What power have we given judgment?

I am honored to be a Certified Facilitator with Access Consciousness®. This body of work is about staying in the question, not having any answers and staying open to the possibilities. One of the mottos is *"A question empowers and an answer disempowers."* If you truly stay in the space of question without expecting any answers, play with what comes in! You will be amazed at what else is possible beyond what you can imagine.

Here are some tips and tricks I have learned from the brilliant creators of Access — Gary Douglas and Dr. Dain Heer and many other fabulous facilitators.

I'd like to offer a game to play — The Barriers Down Game. See if you can get a friend or a few friends to play this with you. Have everyone judge you for a few minutes. Be sure you have your barriers up and defend yourself. These judgments are done silently, not said out loud. Notice the energy and how you feel about what is being projected at you and how your judgers feel.

Next step — lower your barriers. If you've never done this, simply think about dropping your barriers — that's all you have to do. Feel your body relax. Lower your barriers some more. Then ask your friends to judge you again silently for a few minutes. Switch roles with your friends and do the exercise again.

I have done this exercise a few times. The difference in these two options is quite amazing. With the barriers up, you feel the judgments and criticisms' being hurled at you and it is quite uncomfortable. You feel yourself wanting to disappear and you want to defend against what you feel being projected.

When my barriers are lowered, the judgments don't affect me. The other interesting thing is the person directing the judgments when barriers are down have a much harder time coming up with judging thoughts. The energy swirling around is gentle, kind and allowing. Normally by the end of a minute or two, you can't even think of a judgment to hurl at the person receiving. Several times, everyone dissolved into giggling by the end.

Some questions to consider – what would your life look like if you had no point of view you felt you needed to defend for or against? Does that feel expansive and generative? If it feels light and juicy, I recommend exploring this greater. I sense in the space of no judgment, no defending and no resistance — greater is possible. What can occur then?

What if in the energy of defending, you have slammed shut many doors of possibilities? What if that judgment isn't even real? If you make it real, then you choose to defend against the power you have given it. If it is true for you, how have you limited your future?

In the space of no defending and no judging, opportunities open up before you like a flower in bloom. Many paths and options are available. Which one shall you choose first? And what's next? And what's next after that? And so on.

As the title of this book suggests, *The Power of Releasing Judgment* changes the trajectory of your life. It certainly changed my life. The turns and roads I have traveled are quite amazing. The road ahead is full of wonder, excitement and opportunities. Staying in the judgment-free zone allows so much to unfold. When you are in gratitude for someone, there is no room for judgment. Gratitude and judgment cannot exist at the same time. The same is true for allowance. Allowance and judgment don't co-exist. What if allowance is the catalyst that allows you to break free from the chains of judgment?

Would you like to choose the light and expansive way of being for your life? I am so grateful for choosing that for me. My family is appreciative that I chose this as well. Our lives are so much richer and happier. I am joyful to leave behind the heavy armor and embrace lightness. What is left to fear or avoid if you embody the space of allowance? When you are being total allowance, the vulnerability that is present is soft and delicious — you desire to savor every moment and dance with the expansive energy present.

I wonder — when did we stop living in the moment? When did we stop being silly for no reason? Is this only allowed for children? When did we become so serious? If you are judging the people in the restaurant who are laughing loudly and having fun, what are you cutting off in your life? What if we embrace joy like never before? Who would like to be light, brightness and joy with me?

I leave you with more questions — What have you been hiding from yourself and the world based on the judgment of it that you think is so wrong? What if that wrongness really is your strongness? That's a different way to look at all the places you've made yourself wrong.

Sitting around with some friends, one woman was degrading herself and a couple other friends asked her to please stop. I said to her "If you could see yourself as others see you — you would release the bondage of judgment." That also made me realize there might be a few hundred thousand places I've done that in my life. Ouch! I love awareness — once I'm aware, I can change anything and so can you!

What if YOU are the joyful smile and hug someone is looking for? What would it take to TURN YOU UP no matter what anyone says? Who is with me?

What if a life without judgment is true freedom? What would your life look like with total freedom? What could you create and generate with that energy?

What would it be like if we stopped hiding? What joy, potency and infectious happiness can we spread? What allowance can I choose today and every day? What if you pick from the menu of your life and allowance is top on the menu to empower you? What if choosing allowance opens doors beyond your wildest dreams? Allowance is just a choice away!

ABOUT THE AUTHOR

BETSY MCLOUGHLIN

Betsy McLoughlin is a Best-Selling Author of several books, Radio Show Host, Certified Facilitator, and Transformational Coach, a Body Process Facilitator, Right Body for You Taster Facilitator and so much more! Her vibrant personality is the space of no judgment and is the catalyst for quicker success and happiness for her clients.

This creator and magician of magnitude has been featured on The Ask BonBon TV Show, numerous radio shows and tele-summits. Her radio show Imperfect Brilliance can be found on A2Zen.fm

Betsy is also a magical Realtor® who creates ease for her clients. Her calm demeanor, willingness to ask questions outside the box and look for what else is possible creates more opportunities for her clients.

Betsy would love to create new possibilities with you. Are you ready?

Betsy would love to hear from you. You can email her at accessbetsy@gmail.com. Check out her websites at:

www.creatingyumminess.com
and www.imperfectbrilliance.com

CHAPTER 22

THE JOURNEY TO JOY: THROUGH JUDGMENT AND INTO THE LIFE OF MY DREAMS

Adelle King

Judgment is insidious. Everywhere we go, everywhere we look, everything we hear, judgment infiltrates and permeates this reality. It is woven into our language, our education, business and the media... Even our concept of family, support and love is seeped with judgment.

You may be thinking to yourself, 'That sounds a bit dramatic.' Or 'That's a bit of an overstatement.' Or 'Surely people aren't that judgmental.' The thing is, judgment has become so invasive in our world, and even in our inner thoughts, that more often than not, we don't even recognize when we are judging.

For me, realizing where and when I was judging has become the key to getting out of depression, finding my sense of self and creating the life I had only dreamed of. I hope that in sharing the journey I went through and

the tools that helped me navigate the way, it
will shed some light for you in how you can
have more of the life you've been imagining for
yourself. Please know, these tools work even if
you've never dealt with depression or anything
of that nature.

Now bear with me while I get super nerdy for a
moment here.

Did you know that, if you look at the origin of
the word "judgment", or rather "judge" it's actually related to the word doom? It's true.

According to etymonline.com the origin of the
word judge is:

judge (v.)
> c. 1300, "to form an opinion about;
> make a decision,"... The Old En-
> glish word was *deman* (see ***doom***).
> (http://etymonline.com/index.
> php?term=judge&allowed_in_
> frame=0)

and doom:

doom (n.)
> Old English *dom* «law, judgment,
> condemnation,»
> (http://etymonline.com/index.
> php?term=doom&allowed_in_
> frame=0)

So basically, judging is condemning and

dooming you. Every time we judge ourselves or others it's like one more cut, one more knife stabbing us, removing a chunk of our skin, of the very fabric of our being. But what if there's a different possibility available?

When I was in high school, I started to notice that I just wasn't happy. I didn't have a sense of who I was. I was whomever I was standing closest to. I would morph to fit what they desired and required. I'd be what they liked and cut off anything that might be a judgeable offense in their eyes. I made myself as plain and neutral as I possibly could. The stakes were high and the price quickly became more than I could bear.

I was constantly working to see myself through the lens of other people's perspective of me. I was seeking to know me through their eyes. I wanted to define who I was based on what I thought they could see about me, that I couldn't.

What I didn't realize was that in doing this, I was actually judging myself and them. I was peering into their world and trying to discover, *from my perspective*, what they thought of me. Then once I had determined what their opinion of me was, I would either judge that it was good and try to turn up some particular aspect of me and make myself one-dimensional... Or worse, and more often, judge myself as wrong and bad and start shutting down aspects of me and trying to change myself in order to fit into what I had determined someone else thought would be acceptable.

Now, I never asked them if any of these calculations were correct or true. Honestly most of this wasn't even done consciously. I simply know that by the time I was getting my first drivers license I was also thinking about what it would be like to drive my car off a steep hill, into a deep ravine, or hurling into a solid tree. In fact, before I was halfway through college, I had totaled five cars.

From there things got dark. Without going into too much of the depressing details, let me just say that driving cars off the road was just the beginning. I went to college and was surrounded by other kids who were lost and hurting themselves in various ways. One student even hung himself from a tree in the middle of the quad. Me, I was judging myself because I was so apathetic, I didn't have the energy to hurt myself properly. So I judged myself for being too fucked up to even be fucked up correctly. Seriously! How ridiculous is that?

I spent 10 years and thousands of dollars on therapy and anti-depressant medications. I tried different doctors, different types of prescriptions, and different kinds of exercise, meditation, journaling and what have you. There was a little relief from each of these, but I knew there was more and I still didn't have a sense of me or a sense joy in my life. Yet, I kept hoping and kept going through the motions.

I was still in therapy, both group and individual, going to college and working and miserable, when my boyfriend at the time asked me, "Do you realize that you always come out of therapy cranky and angry?"

I hadn't realized, but I started paying attention after that. I noticed that we would start group therapy each week with how we were feeling. Mostly it was, "I'm angry, I'm sad, I'm tired." When something good did happen, saying I'm happy, or hopeful, or excited in that setting was uncomfortable. Then we'd talk about our past and our family, and things we didn't like and couldn't change.

Therapy had given me some strategies and kept me alive through a lot of sadness and struggle, but this was no longer working and I made a demand. I knew where I was, I knew where I wanted to be, and I knew there must be something that could get me from point A to point B in a way that was fun, easy and didn't require stirring the shit and dwelling on the past.

Two weeks later Dr. Dain Heer and Access Consciousness® entered my life. I heard something, I don't even remember what, but it spoke to what I knew I was looking for. It was what I had always known could be and yet always seemed to elude me.

As I delved deeper into the tools of Access Consciousness, I was invited to look at what my points of view were and see them as just an interesting point of view; one of many vantage points for seeing the world and interpreting the events occurring around me. This is much like the 2008 film, *Vantage Point*, where a president is assassinated in the middle of a public square and eight different onlookers have unique information about the crime based on where they were standing at the time of the incident. While they all have distinct information, it doesn't make any one of them right or wrong, they simply have different points of view. In fact, theirs is only one of possibly infinite points of view of what occurred in the square.

A point of view can show up in many ways, the things we like and don't like, who we believe we are and aren't, who we will or won't socialize with, what we can and can't do. These are our opinions, preferences, thoughts, beliefs, feelings, doubts, and fears. The idea behind this concept is that if we have a fixed point of view or judgment about something, it limits us from seeing an incident, or even the world as a whole, in any other way, including sometimes what's actually, truly going on.

For a while, this was a very difficult concept for me to get an understanding of and once I got the concept, I still struggled to apply it. I kept hearing, "Interesting Point of View is where everything is just an interesting point of view." Now I had been taught that you cannot define a term by using that term in the definition, so this explanation simply wasn't working for me. Plus, I was convinced that I didn't know what my point of view was... I didn't even know if I had a point of view. That was part of the problem. At the same time, I kind of thought this tool was about having no preferences at all ever, which I can tell you now, was not correct either.

What I did have were song lyrics that would get stuck in my head. When I'd take a closer look at what the lyrics were, I'd usually discover that they matched what I thought my sentiments about a situation would be. Usually, these were thoughts I was too afraid or unwilling to voice to others. I would swallow my words to avoid offending the people around me. ('Because,' I thought, 'surely if I said what was true for me, at least one person would be offended or disapprove.' This by the way, is a judgment.)

So, for a while, these song lyrics were the closest I could get to having any awareness of my own view of the world. I was still in search of who I was and now I was seeking to know what my outlook of the world was as well. To uncover the deepest darkest judgments I had been hiding from everyone, myself included, because surely they must be heinous and awful. (Another judgment.) And, if they weren't heinous and awful, at the very least, they were holding me back from the life I'd been imagining and knew was possible.

I'd heard other Access Consciousness facilitators talking about being willing look at and
then give up things you've decided, somewhere
along the way, that you have to be or do for
your mother, father, brother, sister or uncle,
in favor of choosing what actually is true for
you and what will work for everyone, including you, in the present moment. They were inviting us to look at what we had decided and
judged our identity to be. The box we had created as who we were.

We do this sometimes at such a young age that
by the time we're adults, we don't even realize it's going on. When we're small a grown up
will tell us, "You're so beautiful / handsome."
"You're a smart cookie." "You'll be a heart-
breaker someday." "You're a good eater." The
list goes on and on. The more we hear these
well-intended comments, the more we begin to
internalize them and become them.

I knew the things people had said about me,
but they didn't ring true in my mind. I knew
there was a gap between what other people saw
and how I felt about myself. And still didn't feel
like I had an identity. If anything, I thought my
identity was stored in some back box, locked
away and hidden far from where anyone could
find it. If I had an identity, if it in fact existed,
it was still a big mystery to me; A secret that
everyone was in on except me.

I was still on the outside of my own life. I realized I had been creating my life as if the things

the people around me desired were the same things I desired. Then I'd find myself disappointed when those same things weren't fulfilling to me.

Even though I had been encouraged to go for what I really desired, a lot of times, the process felt like banging my head against a brick wall or standing at the edge of a cliff with no other choice but to leap to my peril. I would go blank when I heard the question, "What do you truly desire?"

I didn't know what I desired. But I kept asking and I kept going. I would bang my head again and again or teeter on the edge of that cliff. I found that when I kept at it, I'd bang and bang and bang and then I'd go to do it again and something strange would happen. It would be as if the wall just dissolved away into a cloud of smoke. Or the cliff, that once appeared miles high and treacherous, now was just a mere curb that I could step off of.

What changed it from being a wall or a cliff to an open passage or curb? Well, largely it was persistence. The willingness to continue ask, 'What is true for *me*?' 'What do *I* actually desire?' 'What would *I* like to create as *my* life?' and suss out, little by little, what was actually mine and what were the ideas I had picked up and bought from others as mine. Pushing forward with enough persistence, revisiting the same questions enough times, and simply continuing through my daily life, finally,

I'd hear something different, or my perspective would shift or something would click that never had been there before.

For me one big shift came on evening when I was out having a drink with a friend and she said, "Let's play a game." I am an oversized child, so I jumped at the idea of playing a game and asked what she had in mind. She suggested that we pretend to be whoever we desired for the rest of the night. I loved the idea! But, much to my surprise, as options for who I could choose to be flooded into my head, all of a sudden all there were these secondary thoughts of, 'Oh no, I can't do that.' 'That would be too much.' 'It's not ok to be that way!' 'What would people think if I acted like that?'

The game almost ended before it even started. Fortunately, my friend didn't let me off the hook that easily. I decided to impersonate someone whose memoire, *Whip Smart*, I had read a couple years prior. I would be a professional New York City dominatrix; off hours, out to dinner and catching up with her girlfriend. I didn't tell my friend that this persona was based off someone else's real life, so she was impressed at how well I pulled off the act. She kept telling me that the guys sitting at the table next to us were eavesdropping so hard, she thought they were going to fall off their chairs. I gleefully soaked up her feedback!

This game and our evening out got me thinking about how many ways I was judging myself that I hadn't even realized. When I was considering all the possibilities of who I'd like to be, pretend or for real, I saw how many judgments I was using to keep me right where I'd always been. For the first time, I started to see how I was judging me.

Pivotal moments like this can come in so many forms. For me it was a conversation with a friend. Sometimes it's something you see or hear on TV or read in a book or overhear as you're walking down the street, a gift someone gives you out of the blue, or a solitary walk in the great outdoors. These moments of revelation can show up in infinite ways, but however they arrive, once they do, there's no going back. You can't unsee or unhear what's been seen or heard. You're perspective is permanently altered. There's a great episode of the televisions show *How I Met Your Mother,* called "Spoiler Alert" that illustrates this really well. They talk about it like shattering a glass. Once it's broken, it cannot be unbroken.

Now, with this information of all the ways I had been judging myself, my search changed. I went from seeking all the judgments of me to seeking again what I would like my life to be like. 'Who would I like to be in the world?' 'What would be fun for me to do today?' It was no longer just a game, but a way of creating my life. It became the path to get me from Point A to the elusive Point B.

The judgments were and are still there, though

I like to think there may be less of them. Now when I noticed them though, I don't let them stop me. I just keep choosing forward toward what I'd like to create. What I've noticed is, as I choose what will make me happy, the people around me have become more supportive and appreciative of me. I enjoy them more, I enjoy the things I do more and I even have moments when I'm grateful and appreciative of me as well!

It's not perfect. This is just the beginning... well maybe somewhere in the middle. I do know that the less I listen to my judgments and the more I move towards the life I've imagined by choosing what is fun and works for me, the happier I get. The days of fearing the return of my depression are gone, even when I'm having lower days. Where it used to take me weeks or months to get out of a dark mood, now it takes me usually no more than a day or only a few hours. I simply ask myself, 'What's beyond this?' 'What would I like to choose now?' 'What can I be happy about in this moment?' my mood shifts and more and more magic shows up.

Asking these questions allows me to see beyond the darkness. It allows me to shine a light through the abyss that guides me to where I'm headed, where I'd like to go. We all know what's true for us. We do and we always have. What do you truly desire? It's the willingness to ask the question and the courage to pursue it. When things are not fun or not making you happier, it's a good sign, you've veered off track from what is true for you. So, are you willing to keep choosing toward the life of your dreams and be unstoppable, no matter what shows up to try and slow you down?

As a teenager, my favorite band was Third Eye Blind. They are a band based in San Francisco. Then I read a memoir I loved of a guy whose story also took place in San Francisco. I became so curious as to what was going on in San Francisco that all of this creative inspiration I admired was coming out of this one city.

It took me 15 years, but I finally moved across the country. I left behind my family and friends, though I still see them when I'm in New York twice a year for the holidays. I had no job or place to live when I arrived. I knew only one person who lived out here. I'd tell people I was moving and they'd ask if it was for a job or a boyfriend. When I said it was just for fun, I could see the gears in their head crunch to a halt and the wires short circuit and blaze.

It was a moment of courage and daring. Well several ongoing moments. I had to choose it and keep choosing, through doubt and fear, the tears and exhaustion. I've made wonderful friends and am able to work from home in my beautiful apartment that's right in the city. I'm living the life I imagined. So now, the adventure continues.

I look back on my journey and where I've been

and what I've come through and I'm grateful for it all; the good, the bad and the ugly. I've read so many books about people who had gone through depressions and the story was always the same. 'I was depressed, I was depressed, I was depressed, then one day I was better!' None of the authors ever shed any light on how exactly they miraculously got better.

So here is what it took for me to go from depression to joy, from feeling lost and confused to having a sense of me and feeling confident about who I am. More importantly, here is what *you* can do, if you'd like to start transforming your life:

- Get clear on what you desire, not what your mom or dad, family or friends desire for you or expect of you. Actually, get clear on what they desire for and from you too, so when those things come up, you can be aware and make choices that will work for you. Which brings us to step two...

- Have the courage and daring to choose the things that will make you happy and lead to more of the life you've been dreaming of. This does not mean treading on the people around you to make it happen. Would doing that actually make you happy? Choosing for you includes what will work for everyone, *including you!*

- Keep going, keep choosing, even when

it feels like banging your head against a brick wall or like you'll go insane or fall off a cliff if you take one more step. It may feel that way some times. Take that next step, keep going, phone a friend who you know is supportive, go for a walk in nature. Do something, do anything, just don't give up!

- Ask questions, always ask questions.

Some of my favorites to ask when I'm feeling low (in no particular order) are:

- What's beyond this?
- What would I like to choose now?
- What can I do now that will create the future I'd like to be living?
- What can I choose to be happy about in this moment?
- What am I grateful for?
- What's right about me/this that I'm not getting?
- What question can I ask that would change this?

Some of my favorite questions to ask when things are going great (also in no particular order) are:

- How does it get infinitely better than this?
- What else is possible now?
- What would it take for more of this to

show up?

- And all of the questions above!

Thank you for going on this journey with me. Please take these tools and use them however they work for you. I'm grateful for you. For you reading this story, seeking and choosing and doing the best that you can with the tools that are available to you.

I am so grateful for the amazing people who have guided me along the way, for these questions, which are some of the tools of Access Consciousness; it's founder, Gary Douglas and Co-creator, Dr. Dain Heer as well as the amazing Facilitators who have all been a contribution to me along the way. Thank you to my family and friends, and the therapists and psychologists who did their best when that was all I had. I'm grateful for me, for the choices I made and some of the choices I didn't make (like choosing to end my life)... Now, what can you choose that will make you happier?

ABOUT THE AUTHOR

ADELLE KING

Adelle is a transformational coach and body worker, who uses the tools of Access Consciousness in classes and private sessions to facilitate her clients to get out of pain and suffering and into their strength and joy to create the life of their dreams. She also has a MS.Ed in Early Childhood and Childhood Education and is certified teacher working for the Access Possibilities School online. Born in Israel and raised in New York, she now resides in San Francisco. She retains her childlike wonder, still believing in fairies, magic and sparkly things. As well as enjoying more refined pleasures like cooking healthy, decadent meals, dancing and traveling to explore everything life has to offer. Her target is to create more joy and laugher in the world anywhere she goes.

CHAPTER 23

STOPPING THE CYCLE OF GUILT, SHAME, FEAR AND ANGER

Ashley Stamatinos

When you're dealing with guilt, shame, fear or anger, it can be suffocating and bring you to a place where you feel like you'll be stuck in this endless cycle with no hope of freeing yourself from its grips. This destructive loop can run deep, but I've found a way to step out of the cycle and free you from these limiting and distracting emotions.

These emotions are designed to disconnect you from your awareness and keep you from seeing the choices you have available. We always have choices, so anytime you feel like something or someone is cornering you and there seems to be no choices, that's a red flag.

When you are experiencing these limiting feelings, those emotions are a blanket that covers up your ability to clearly see what's going on and what's possible. They are "distracting" you from what's REALLY going on all around you and they stop you from seeing how you have the power to change your situation.

Where I stand right now, I no longer have any of those distracting emotions in my life. I figured out how to remove them anytime they *show their face*, and you can do the same.

In fact, I can see guilt a mile away, and I now have that space to choose to allow it into my world or not. Of course, I choose to not let it in.

I am no longer suffocating underneath the blanket of those limiting emotions, and let me tell you, the view from here is wonderful! When you're immersed in guilt, shame, fear or anger, it's hard to see that you can free yourself from those shackles.

You may think it's really hard and it takes a lot of work to remove guilt, shame, fear or even anger from your life, but what if it didn't have to be hard? What if I gave you a few simple practical tools to step out of the cycle? Are you ready to break free and remove those suffocating emotions now?

There are two specific tools I use which always work for me and these tools have worked for the thousands of people I've shared the tools with to date. I can best share these tools with you by giving you examples of how I've successfully used the tools in my own life.

Removing the Heavy Cloud of Guilt

Have you ever left a social gathering feeling

worse than when you arrived? Frequently, highly aware people feel social anxiety around groups of other people.

Even if you like being social, sometimes going out and being with a large group can bring on a wave of emotions that can feel debilitating.

I have a large extended Greek family and we have many social gatherings. I used to feel very uncomfortable joining in on these gatherings when the entire family would get together. Of course, no one really picked up on my discomfort, because I was all smiles on the outside.

I remember a particular party that I attended a few years ago that was particularly problematic. As I was getting ready to go to the event, I was feeling great; I liked how I felt; I was happy with what I was wearing; and I was proud of the way my life was going at that moment in time.

I walked into this family gathering and within the first 30 minutes I wanted to put my jacket back on to hide myself. Then I started to replay in my head the things I had just said in conversations, to make sure I hadn't actually said anything stupid or unkind. I started wondering to myself if I had bragged about an accomplishment while talking with someone or if I had simply talked too much during an exchange with a family member. I kept re-thinking what may have caused this and what I might have done.

It was so strange to be so full of conflicting emotions and thoughts with all of them weighing me down, making me feel even heavier and very tired.

Then the pesky guilt started creeping in. I started feeling badly about everything. It was the kind of guilt that was non-specific. I couldn't really put my finger on why I felt guilty; I just was feeling like I had done something wrong.

At this point, all of these oppressive emotions and thoughts were swirling around in my head at such speed that they were making me actually dizzy. Luckily the party was about over, so I did a quick sweep through the party to say goodbye and walked out to my car to center myself.

As my husband drove us home, I started going through a kind of checklist in my head as I tried to find the source of the nagging guilt I was feeling.

Because of this guilt, I felt like I was in a foggy, dark cloud. The cloud had weight and texture. It felt as if it would suffocate me if I didn't address it and then somehow remove it.

After sorting through all the possible causes of how I may have created this guilt by doing something wrong, I realized there was no real reason for blaming myself. I couldn't think of any real reason I should be feeling guilty!

That's when I remembered to ask myself a question. I asked, "Does this guilt belong to me?"

And whoosh, I felt as though a gust of wind passed through me taking away half of that dark cloud of guilt and the heavy weight I had felt. What a relief!

Most of our thoughts, feelings and emotions don't originate from us. This was a prime example of just that. The guilt I was feeling did not belong to me. I knew it didn't belong to me, because when I asked if it was mine, I immediately felt a sense of relief. That relief is the indicator that the emotion wasn't yours.

If you ask, "Does this belong to me?" and you feel heavier, and then the emotion settles deeper within you, that's when you know you actually created it. A little hint though, it is very rare that you created the limiting thought, feeling or emotion.

We all go our whole lives picking up the thoughts, feelings, emotions and points of view of those around us and it takes us further away from feeling centered and grounded in our true self.

Now that I had asked the question and gained an awareness that the guilt wasn't mine, I was feeling a bit better, but I still had a little more work to do so I could feel like myself again.

I felt relief from asking if the guilt was mine, so I followed that up by saying to myself, "I return you to sender." (You could also simply say, "I release you and let you go," or whatever feels best for you.)

The guilt I was feeling was quickly dissipating and I didn't even need to know who it came from in order to release it and feel better. Just knowing that it wasn't mine allowed me to find relief and let it go.

I was also still feeling strange about my body, and so I asked myself, "Is this guilt and shame I'm feeling about my body that makes me want to cover it up and hide it, belong to me?" I heard a big loud, "NO!" And immediately I felt a sense of relief, allowing me to feel very clear that no, that guilt and shame I was feeling about my body was not mine to carry.

I said, "I release you and let you go!" The dark cloud of guilt, which had engulfed me, was dissipating and I was feeling great relief, but I wasn't feeling completely like myself again, yet.

I did a little checklist beginning by asking myself, "What else feels uncomfortable right now?" My attention was drawn to how I had been feeling a sense of worry, wondering if I had said anything in the party that was bragging or unkind.

So, of course, I asked myself, "Did I really say

anything unkind or inappropriate?" and immediately my gut / my intuition told me, "NO."

So again, I said, "I release all those feelings of worry."

The cloud had lifted fully now, and I was back. I looked over at my husband and said "Hi." He said, "Nice to have you back."

I realized that when I go into social gatherings, I am so hyper-aware that I was picking up on everyone's insecurities, worries, fears, feelings of guilt and even shame.

It can be very uncomfortable if you allow them to pile up like I did, but it's no longer like that for me. I catch them before they soak into me as a limitation.

Every time I feel a discomfort or as if I'm not being myself, I immediately ask myself, "Does that belong to me?" and then I let it go. I ask myself this quite often and it allows me to differentiate between what's mine and what belongs to other people.

I no longer need to carry their judgments and limiting points of view as if they were mine. I see them as they come into my awareness and then I choose to not let them become my way of functioning.

Not allowing yourself to be suffocated by a cloud of guilt, shame, anger or blame is a simple question followed up by a choice to let it go and not carry it around.

A Gift Wrapped in Judgment

The day before the birth of our child, we received devastating news that someone very close to us had just been diagnosed with inoperable Stage IV cancer.

This isn't a story about his cancer; thankfully, he is healthy and thriving now.

This relative lived in New York, and my husband and I live in Chicago, so we could not be with him at the time he was going through treatments. He went through radiation and chemotherapy for many months.

This relative also needed time to focus on himself and make his healing his biggest priority. Because of his treatments and how far away he lived from us, he wasn't able to meet our child until he was about six months old.

I remember when our child was five months old, I had a friend over to my home. As we were chatting and catching up, she asked me if my husband's family in New York was in love the new baby in the family. Without missing a beat, I said, "Yes, of course! They love chatting on video with him frequently."

My friend was confused and asked me, "Wait, you mean they haven't come out here to see all of you yet?"

I replied, "Well, no. They have a lot going on and they couldn't make it out here yet because of health issues."

She seemed irritated for some reason and said to me, "No matter how sick I was I would fly anywhere to see the new baby in the family when they were born. Aren't you mad that they haven't seen him in person yet?"

At this point, I felt a wave of anger rise from deep within me. It was like in a split second, everything slowed down and I could sense a stressful feeling within me come up from my feet and rise into my head clouding my thoughts.

I paused and didn't go into reaction.

Still, within this slow motion space, I quickly asked myself a question, "If I wasn't angry right now, what would I be aware of?"

That energy that had risen from my feet all the way into my head started to move back down and out of my head. I felt my headspace clear a little and I had a tiny space for being aware of what was going on.

I asked the question again, "If I wasn't angry right now, what would I be aware of?" and I saw clearly that this friend of mine wasn't trying to make me angry or offend. Her intention wasn't even to judge our relatives for their actions; what she was trying to do is be a supportive friend to me.

She thought that her judgments would be a good connection point for us and that maybe if she pointed out all the injustices she saw, that I would jump on the judgment train with her and it would make me feel she was being a good supportive friend.

Many times friends will connect with judgments instead of connecting with thoughts and ideas about what's possible and how to create a greater world or a greater life. It's much more common for people to fall into connecting by judging others. It's simply a choice to connect from a space of creating instead of connecting from a space of judging.

So, I'm in this split second pause. I felt the anger and stress rise within me and then I asked a question. The emotions that were clouding my space started to dissipate and I received some clarity and space to see what was going on in front of me.

I realized that my friend was trying to connect with me by judging our relative and his choices. Her judgments immediately put me into reaction mode and brought out anger within me.

That choice I made to ask a question, allowed me to have greater awareness. I was now able to see I had a larger space available where I could make another choice. Do I let out this anger and react by defending our relative?

I asked myself quickly, "What's really going on here?"

That's when I realized that my friend was being giving in her own way, and I almost missed the gift in her actions. She was offering me support by way of judgment. I almost missed it because it's not really how I function, and it's not the way I offer support to people any longer.

I had another choice here, receive her gift or reject her gift?

In that slowed down moment of question, choice and awareness, I realized that the kindest thing to do was to move past the anger and see what was really going on here. I chose to receive her gift by thanking her for her support.

When I thanked her and continued the conversation, I didn't point out her judgments; I didn't judge along with her or defend or react to her words; I simply acknowledged that she was being supportive (in her way), and I was in allowance of her way of being supportive to me.

From this space of awareness, it's like you have a *bird's eye view* of the interactions taking place. You can see the exchanges from a different perspective and catch subtleties that would most likely be missed without choosing to ask a question.

When you don't ask, "If I wasn't angry, what would I be aware of?", that anger will creep up and blind you from being able to be aware and you might miss the gifts that are right in front of you.

Often the gifts people are offering come wrapped up in packaging that is misleading, and without the question to see beyond their colorful packaging, you will miss the kindness that people are offering you in the best way they know how to offer them.

What I'm illustrating to you is also how to be in allowance of others. Allowing them to be who they are, in the best way they know how to be, without judging them.

Allowance is void of judgment. When you allow others to gift you in the best way they know how, you will not be soaking in their judgments and points of view, the kindness will fill you up and those judgments will pass right by you without impacting you.

That's the beauty of being in allowance.

If you pair asking questions to gain greater awareness and being in allowance (or non-judgment) of others, you are setting yourself up for a much smoother ride in your life.

I challenge you to remove the belief that change needs to be met with challenge or difficulty. Although these teachings I'm offering seem simple, they are potent enough to change even the deepest guilt, shame, fear or anger if you use implement them consistently.

Now that you have the tools to change anything within your life, what will you choose? Don't breeze over these tools and forget about them, be sure to write them down and reference them as often as possible. Isn't it time to get out of old patterns that are no longer working for you and start creating a life you love?

About the Author

ASHLEY STAMATINOS

Ashley is the co-author of numerous #1 bestselling books, including "The Energy of Expansion," "The Energy of Spirit" and "The Energy of Healing." She is widely known as the Empath Expert for her extensive work with highly sensitive people, and she is an international speaker.

She has been interviewed on TV multiple times for her work with highly sensitive individuals. Her mission is to give you the tools to find lasting inner peace within your busy life.

Ashley is the founder of Omorfi Healing, a business that she created as a platform to offer holistic education and healing to the world. She is passionate about teaching, and has been teaching for the last 10+ years. Within her practice she offers private coaching and both online and in-person courses to those seeking to create a life they love.

Are you wondering if you're an Empath? Take the free *Am I an Empath? Quiz* on the home page of Ashley's website, OmorfiHealing.com.

If you feel drawn to working further with Ashley on a one-on-one basis, you can go to her website and apply for a **Free 30 Minute Clarity Call**. (OmorfiHealing.com)

Ashley travels to guest lecture and teach her specialty classes. If you'd like her to come to your business to teach a course or to give a guest lecture, please email info@omorfihealing.com for further information.

Get Social with Ashley:

Facebook.com/OmorfiHealing

Instagram.com/OmorfiHealing

Twitter.com/OmorfiHealing

YouTube.com/OmorfiHealing

Pinterest.com/OmorfiHealing

Periscope.tv/OmorfiHealing

www.OmorfiHealing.com

CHAPTER 24

JUDGMENT SCHMUDGMENT

Erika James

Did you reject your own knowing?

For me, self-judgment began in childhood. My first addiction, I suppose. Being a highly aware being, I perceived the truth behind a situation from a very early age. I did not know that is what I was doing, I just knew when things felt twisty and off, even though everyone was dressed nicely and smiling. Growing up in a dysfunctional family that had lots of love and also lots of drama and trauma, it was clear that things were not as we were pretending them to be. We were in full denial of reality. When I asked questions, I was told everything was fine (it wasn't), that we were all happy and normal (we weren't), and that I was too sensitive and was imagining things (yes, I was sensitive and no, I was not imagining things). So basically it was conveyed to me verbally and non-verbally, that everything I saw, felt, and knew was totally wrong. Being the smart girl that I am, I realized quickly that I depended on these people for love, food, shelter – for everything. My solution was that I had better stop asking questions and just try to be more like them, and life would be easier. I judged everyone around me as the ones who were right about everything, and judged myself and my instinct as not trustworthy and confusing.

This was the beginning of my doubting my truth and my knowing. Enter therapy and the self-improvement books and studies over the next decade, and I had confirmation that there was something wrong with me and I needed fixing. I was given labels and diagnoses to even make it official and shameful. I judged myself inferior and judged everyone else as superior. With this pattern of shrinking and contracting, my essence became more and more hidden over time.

Where the heck is that memo?

It seemed to me that everyone else in the world was given this elusive, magic memo called "How to Do Life". Apparently, this memo had detailed instructions and gave everyone else the secret to being successful and happy. Why did I not get this memo too? WTF? And so, I began my quest to seek the answers that everyone else seemed to have been given at birth. In my search for answers, I gave my personal power away to therapists, coaches, boyfriends, a husband (now my wasband), peers, my parents, etc. I figured they all must know more about me than I did, because they seemed to not feel the need to seek and improve themselves like I did. Therefore, they were just naturally happy and must have the answers. And all these people never had a shortage of opinions on what I should be doing according to their reality. So, they must know better than I! Guess what? They did not know anything about me. This may sound like common sense to most folks out there, but it took me awhile to truly GET this.

I AM THE ONLY EXPERT ON ME.

YOU ARE THE ONLY EXPERT ON YOU.

WHAT IS RIGHT ABOUT YOU THAT YOU ARE NOT GETTING?

Exercise:
Ask a Question!

Is this judgment, conclusion, emotional upset really true?

What else can I choose in this situation?

Is this mine? (VERY likely it's not even yours, it's something you picked up from someone else)

What can I be, do, feel, think differently about this situation that I am not aware of yet?

Comparing Your Insides to Other People's Outsides

Comparison and judgment are one and the same. When my kids were little, my life was chaos. They were born 15 months apart. I had a huge home and I tried to do it all with no help. No cleaning lady, no babysitter. I expected that since I was a stay-at-home mom, I should be able to do it all myself. And I expected that I do it perfectly like everyone else in our perfect upper class Midwestern subdivision seemed to do. My dear friend and neighbor across the street seemed to have the perfect life. She had time to lunch with friends, workout, sit and read books, host parties, etc. She had older kids and also was smart enough to have help. When I would go over to her house, I would judge her a better wife and mother because her house seemed perfect and she would cook delicious meals for her family three nights a week or more. When I went to her house all I saw was what I was failing at, and so I figured she knew how to be a good mother, a good wife. I did not factor in that she had help. I did not factor in that she had already lived through her "boot camp" time as she called it. She had already lived through the days of young babies and frazzled mom nerves. I did not factor in that she has strengths that were different than mine. I just looked at her outside life and judged myself on the inside. I stopped myself finally and asked, "What is right about ME that I am not getting?" I realized, she had her own way to do things, her own strengths, which were completely different than mine. That it is counter-intuitive to try to do things any other way than what works for me. I realized that I needed to look at my strengths, and work WITH myself instead of against myself. I had a choice. I could choose to stop assuming I was "wrong" and choose to begin to do things in my funky creative way that worked just perfectly for me. Acknowledging that I have my own strengths, and building on them, rather than tearing myself down with comparison.

It's a waste of energy to focus on what you think you are not good at and spend all your time trying to improve what perhaps just is not your strongest capacity. Do ducks feel bad about themselves for not being a squirrel and spend their time work on being better at climbing trees instead of joyfully swimming about with ease? Do squirrels stop climbing trees to try to swim and spend all their energy feeling ashamed for not being better swimmers? No. They just be themselves, and do what they are innately good at doing. Take your strengths, and work WITH them. Create your own unique way to do things, based on what works with you. Look at what is RIGHT about you. Stop looking at what you have judged as wrong about you. Please. Stop.

Exercise:
Ask a Question!

When you compare yourself to others and start feeling that you are not good enough or just not good in general. Ask these questions:

Who does this thought/feeling/emotion belong to? Is this mine?

What is right about me that I am not getting?

What capacities do I have here that I am I refusing to be aware of, that if I was aware of would bring the change that I am desiring?

What unlimited choice do I have in every situation, that IF I CHOSE IT, would change ALL reality?

Listen to your body and your feelings. They are your internal guidance system.

Our bodies are giving us feedback all the time. When we are living and choosing thoughts that are what we DO wish to have in our lives, our bodies feel amazing and light. Think about how great it feels in your body on those days where you're in sync with what you desire to be creating in your life. It feels wonderful. When you surround yourself with people who contribute to you and are in vibration with your higher self, it's easy and you come away from them feeling expanded and light. When you are doing things you love that contribute to your life, it's expansive. It truly is very simple. Follow and foster these feelings, choose these thoughts, choose to be around people like this as much as possible. That happy and joyful feeling is guiding you to know what is true for you. The more you choose what brings a smile upon your face and makes you happy, the more those situations will show up in your life.

Listen to the discomfort and the unpleasant feelings inside. The stronger the discomfort the bigger the indicator is that you are getting further from what matches with who you truly BE. The more it hurts, the bigger the gap between where you would like to be and where you are at in that moment. The discomfort is VALUABLE info! Listen to it! Clear everything around it that is blocking you from choosing what you do want instead! Whether you stay in a job that you dread going to every day, or hang around people who judge your dreams and try to keep you small to fit in with their beliefs, or stay in that relationship out of duty even though it feels like you are dying inside, it feels terrible. Your body's discomfort is a clear indication that you are living with discordant situations that are not anything close to what you truly desire in your life.

Exercise:
Ask a Question!

If I continue to choose this _____, what will my life be like in five years?

(Does it make you feel like puking? Or does it feel like someone just poured champagne down your crown chakra and your whole body lit up?) You will know the answer. It's your choice what you then decide to choose.

What else can I choose here that I am not yet aware of? (You may not get an answer but it will begin to bring you new possibilities just by asking the question.)

Pay attention to signs that you are ignoring your internal guidance system

As a kid, this choking down my knowing and judging myself as less-than showed up in my body as headaches and stomach aches. Later, it became that dull ache and ever-present knot in my stomach that I learned to live with and it became normal for my insides to be churning and eating away at my body. As a young adult I began to try to ignore the soul splitting pain of going against myself all the time by drinking alcohol more and more often to make it tolerable. The addiction of self-judgment can show up in other forms as well. Over the years I have turned to eating disorders, alcohol, abusive relationships with men, excessive shopping, excessive exercising, and more to help release the pressure of the pain that was the non-stop critical mind and judgment in my head. None of it worked. I have become an expert on quitting self-destructive behaviors. The judgment in my head is the root of all of those outward behaviors. It all starts in your head. Using these tools to release the judgment will allow you to loosen your death grip on the addictions and self-defeating habits and you will be able to move out of the "stinkin' thinkin'" more quickly as you replace it with focusing on what you DO wish to have in your life.

Other ways ignoring your internal guidance signals can appear in your life could be physical pain and illnesses, sex addictions, over working, blaming others/being a victim, prescription drugs or street drugs, depression, and so forth.

Exercise:

Begin to be aware and notice your body's reactions to your thoughts, situations, and to people. Listen carefully to how you feel in every area of your life. When it feels uncomfortable and heavy- STOP doing whatever it is that is bringing that feeling into your life. If it's a whisper of a wonky feeling about a decision you are about to make, ask some questions. *"If I choose this, will it contribute to my life?" "If I choose this, will my life will be better in five years?"* The more you do this, the easier it will become. It will become automatic to do right away the more you get used to feeling light and choosing that which is what you DO want in your life.

Your thoughts, feelings, points of view are your internal energetic Google

So what's the big deal about being aware of your judgments about yourself and others, and why should you care to change them? Consider this: our brains are the most powerful search engines in the world, much more powerful than Google or any others. What are you doing when you type in a word in the search area of Google and click "search"? You are asking for anything related to that word to be brought to you. And what does Google do when you click that search button? Google goes out, scours the entire internet universe, and in milliseconds, brings you back all possible items related to your search. Ask and you shall receive.

Your thoughts do the same thing. Your point of view creates your reality. Now what I am going to say next may make you angry. Good. *Everything you are living in your life is a response to the story of the judgments you are telling yourself.* Every time you think and speak these stories, they go out and bring more of the same to you. If you want to start living the life you would really like to be having, then you have to start telling the new story of your life as the life the way you want it to be. Then, your search engine will begin to actualize around what you DO desire in your life. The more your thinking revolves around critical thoughts, or judgments of anything, the more you bring more of just that into your reality. Judgments only give you one solid point of view; they eliminate anything else being able to come into your thoughts as a possibility. Be totally honest with yourself. How much do you focus on what you do not want in your life? What your husband, your mother, your kids, your friends etc. are not doing right, who you are mad at, who looked at you funny, etc. What kind of searches are you sending out into the Universal Energetic Google of your reality?

Exercise:

Do not tell the old story of what is not working in your life anymore. Stop yourself from
thinking about it. Change your thinking and
talking to being all about the life you DO desire to be living. Sit with it. Hold the thought
and images of what you do wish to have in
your life and hold it for as long as you can.
Hold it for 20 seconds. Then 30 seconds. Then
minutes. Imagine it in detail. Smell it. Taste it.
Then continue to build on that and do longer
and longer each as often as possible. Once a
day at least. Keep doing this and do not give
up. You are building new thinking muscles, so
give them time to develop. You will begin to see
new things show up in your life. Give it time.
All your years of old thoughts are still trickling
in, do not judge what shows up and just keep
asking for what else is possible. And just when
you think nothing is changing, and you are
about to give up, dig your heels in and keep
going. This is the point when you are about
to flip your switch, when it feels like nothing
is happening. It is beginning to change, so
please, do not stop.

Go slow to go fast

Begin to be patient with yourself. Now I say
"beginning" to change everything because if
you are anything like me, you really would like
everything to change with a snap of your fin-
gers and POOF it's done. As a retired expert
in getting in my own way and doing things the

hard way, I am telling you to start slow. Plowing through information via books, classes, coaches, basically becoming a hoarder of self-help tools can actually slow you down. The cycle of judgmental thoughts will continue and you'll then add to it the judgment of you for not being better, changing faster, using the tools better, etc.

Slow down, get some grip on the wheel of your life, and start to turn your ship in a different direction. Give it time to change course. You are changing more than you know or see.

All these thoughts and patterns have been going on for a long time in our minds. IT WILL TAKE SOME TIME FOR THE NEW WAYS OF BEING TO BECOME PART OF YOU. Be patient with yourself. Go slow to go fast. Meaning, if you slow down to take time on these critical foundational tools, you will be creating change faster down the road. Trying to rush the process will trip you up. Also, if you are used to "efforting" at things to somehow feel as if you are really working hard at it so it should change faster, STOP IT. Efforting is an illusion that actually will slow your change down. Feeling your way into the higher vibrational pattern is what will change things. Use two to three tools your first two weeks or so. Use the same three as often as you can remember and then patiently observe what new things begin to change. Acknowledge what is changing. Look at where you started and where you are at each week. Celebrate the changes. And

think on them. Think on what it is you desire to BE and what life you are living. Enjoy
the process, the journey, the ride. Be grateful
for every breath you take and for the gift you
BE. You are a beautiful being. Love yourself
and enjoy your evolution.

About the Author

ERIKA JAMES

Erika James is a brilliantly intuitive and gifted life coach with the touching capacity to be the mirror for people to see who they truly BE. She targets on the elimination and eradication of all the lies that have been bought to cloud her client's vision of themselves. Erika can go to the deepest depths with her clients and help them see the gift and the beauty of where they have been, and then take them to the highest peaks of possibility. Erika utilizes powerful coaching techniques and training to assist those willing and ready to change to take off into the next dimension of living the life they dream of living. Erika's rich background and expertise in many areas of personal development contribute to her client in creating epic changes in relationships, professional life coaching, sex/sensuality/sexuality, body acceptance, self esteem, addictions and more. She effectively guides her clients away from swimming upstream and doing things the hard way, and towards self-love and self-acceptance to create an authentic life of ease and joy. She is a Tony Robbins Certified Coach, an Internationally Certified Scientific Hand Analyst, an Access Consciousness Bars Facilitator and Bodyworker.

CHAPTER 25

DANCING WITH JUDGMENT
A Poem

Cass Hepburn

Lately I have been
Pondering about judgment.
And where and how
I learned to be the judge and jury of my life.
I had really great teachers at home.
At school,
An abusive teacher
the bullies who came after.
The Lovers,
The envious.
Those who assumed
That my outward appearance
Gave them a reason
To love or hate me.
So much judgment
And I believed it
As I desperately resisted against it.
I allowed myself to shrink
To make others more comfortable
To avoid being a target

All the while hiding it away
Into the recesses of my body
My mind,
My Being.
My Ms Sunshine outlook on life
Is not what ran on the inside
And I locked and hid all these boxes away
Well beyond the sight of anyone
Other than perhaps a rare glimpse
To an insightful friend.
Willing to look
A little closer.
I became a chameleon who could blend into
many environments
but couldn't feel comfortable in my own skin.
My world narrowed into a tiny space
That was hard to take breath in.
And whether it was an answer
to a prayer whispered in a moment of
desperation
Or a demand for more
I found tools
That helped me find the keys
to unlock the boxes
Of my self-made jail.
It is still a voyage of discovery
amidst the clutter
Of dress-up clothes
In the attic
To find who exactly it is
Who lies here within
These invisible, now permeable walls.

About the Author

CASS HEPBURN

I grew up at a time that judgment was a measurement of our society. My family like many others was filled with it. As was school and church. For me however the person I always judged most harshly was myself. Through my life I made choices that both attracted criticism towards me and gave me more fuel to judge myself.

Then thankfully I began to learn and explore others ways to live, that were so much kinder.

I saw the family patterns that contributed to certain behaviours and I worked with those. I began to choose friends and partners who cared for me and were kind but who would also call bullshit when it was called for.

I explored alternative healing and began learning techniques not just for myself but also to use with others as well. I began teaching Reiki classes and worked in the healing, bodywork and aromatherapy field.

A few years ago I came across Access Consciousness® and these tools have enabled me to let go of the deep sense of wrongness that I had held for so long and given my life so much ease.

Judgment is no longer my constant companion and I am able to see the beauty and wonder that is this beautiful planet that we are so blessed to get to play and live upon.

And I am filled with gratitude.

CHAPTER 26

QUIET THE INNER CRITIC

Erica Marie Glessing

Suspending judgment is the first step to being joyful, expansive, alive, and awakening to my inner power and strength.

I'm not always able to quiet the inner critic, and when I don't, I suffer. When I listen to the judgments of others as a way of guidance for my choices, the results are not pretty.

The first judgments heaped at me "You are too smart." "You are too pretty." Then later "You are too fat. You will never make it because you are too fat." "You are never going to make it because..."

The lies serve a role that keeps you small. Are you ready to bust lies? What if each day, you wake up, and agree to bust one lie open and expose it for the lie that it is?

For example, what if you are not wrong for the choice you made yourself wrong about. Who has chosen a job that didn't work out, chosen a lover who cheated, chosen a rotten-to-the-core co-parent? Who has chosen to think small instead of choosing to expand into the awareness of the light and beautiful being you are? I have done most of those things and I am in the most amazing life right now, that defies all logic for the magic it is.

I have the kind of magic where if I'm walking in the aisle in a grocery store that is crowded beyond measure, and ask for a grocery cart in my mind's eye (if I decide mid-stream to have a cart instead of a basket), a cart shows up within about 10 seconds.

Same with the love of my life, he showed up as if by magic. The house (I live in a dream house) didn't show up as if by magic until it did show up, as if by magic. I mean, the right house took me some time, but I did this one shift where I just said WHATEVER IT TAKES I AM IN and then the next weekend it showed up.

Bursting the Lies
You Didn't Recognize as Lies

What lies were you told as a child? Reflect on lies possibly well-meaning grandparents, parents, teachers, and brothers or sisters might have told you lies. Especially those lies motivated by jealousy or awe. Were you too much? Too happy? Too exuberant? Did you have too much energy? Most children when tended will have too much energy, will push the envelope on the rules, and will do their best to break free of chains that parents place upon them.

I also find this with animals, for instance, happy loved horses tend to be curious and push against the walls of the rules. Unhappy broken-spirited horses will obey the rules. So when a horse gets imaginative, I like to reward them for being happy and also guide them to be safe, especially if I'm riding them at the time. So I show them how to be happy and silly and also be safe, and this is a great recipe for life in general.

To get to the place where you are free to recognize the lies, you could embark upon a journey of awareness that begins with a question (well it ends with lots more questions too) but it begins with maybe a simple question.

What do I believe about me that if I could release would change everything?

What lies were I told that if I could recognize them would open up my world, and then open it up again, and then again?

What gifts do I have that were named as problems? Could I see my capacities as gifts and joy and release the need to see the world through eyes of "being wrong" all the time?

Expansion verses Contraction

You can tell something is a lie about you if it makes you experience smallness, contraction, a pain in your stomach, a place of "no power" as opposed to full power and expansion.

The saying "the truth will set you free" resonates big for me, I don't know about you. The truth or an expansive concept of a being as connected to all that is, and capable of all that could become, is more true than contractive thoughts of "I can't change this," that's one of the biggest lies running on people for hundreds of thousands of years.

Change is Constant

Have you ever had a major epiphany and then everything in your world had to change? One morning I woke up and said "I would like an epiphany today." I can't remember the details but I got one, and it was a good one. How funny! I just asked and then I had in my mind's eye an epiphany and it changed everything.

What have you let jail you or keep you down that you are ready to release? Is there something you've believed, a lie you have held close? Is there a place inside of you where you don't trust your value?

You Matter

One morning I was standing in line at the dollar store near my house. A man walked in and he was dressed, he was spotless, he had a fresh haircut, and he had clearly spent some time in the gym the last few months. He walked like he knew himself, and he grinned at everyone – he smiled a big smile and people around him felt that and smiled back.

I looked into the parking lot and saw a woman wearing dark clothes with a veil covering her hair. She was shuffling through the parking lot, she was possibly in her 60s or 70s. She had possibly had disappointment heaped on her body every day for 20 or 30 years. She was one of the unhappiest people I've ever observed. The sorrow brimmed over and spilled into the rainy parking lot and emanated out even further.

In that moment, with those two people perfectly juxtaposed like bookends, I saw how much each person matters. My smile matters. My way of being matters. When I overcome a major obstacle, it matters. Staying clear and happy in my own skin, this matters.

A Willingness to Shine

A lot of people get stuck on being willing to shine. Being willing to shine is about releasing judgment on yourself, and also, releasing judgment of others, and also, releasing judgment of your parents, and releasing judgment of anyone who ever judged you to be less than.

Do you walk into a room and see others as more valuable than you? Do you take classes from people you have chosen to make choices for you because of their brilliance?

I had a brilliant conversation the other day with one of my favorite authors and editors, and she asked me where I had decided I was less than anyone else.

You are born into this body during this lifetime – you are a gift. Are you celebrating the gift that you are? Could you celebrate more, this being you are?

Letting Go

There is a documentary called "Letting Go" and it is a simple concept. In the documentary, thousands of instances of "letting go" are revealed. The star of the show (the show is about the Sedona method) holds a pen and lets it go. If you are holding onto something, or someone, or someplace, it could be that your spirit is calling you to let it go.

I have let go of more baggage than I ever imagined I was even carrying. Yet, as a sensitive, I am able to get lots more new baggage every day if I choose. I can walk into a grocery store and "grasp" the thoughts of everyone around me. I am able to be at the hockey rink during a tournament and sense all the parent's desires heaped on the backs of their kids. Hockey parents carry around a little judgment. Hockey parents think about what should be done right and how to be a right hockey parent. Each has judgments about the coach and some have lots of judgments about the other players.

Some of the young players, even at say age seven or eight, might have judgments about their fellow players and how hard or not hard their teammates are working at their "job" of playing hockey.

Even when I say it, I can hear how silly that sounds. So, when my daughter (guess what, she is also sensitive) has a bad game, she feels the disappointment heaped upon her little shoulders. She feels it too, but how much of what she is experiencing in her body is hers, and how much is the rest of the team or the other parents or the coaches?

So, if you, like me, can walk into a room and leave with lots of baggage, what could you choose instead? What could you be without all of that on your shoulders? Could you walk out of a room without all their baggage?

Awareness helps, so much. Any time you begin to get a sick-to-your-stomach sensation, you are possibly picking up judgment from others.

I find that a ritual helps. What have I picked up today that I don't choose to keep in my head, body, heart, life? Imagine if you pick things up every single day and then keep them in your body, and they have no way out.

Judgment Can Make You Sick

One of my family friends was having a lot of trouble with migraines. I looked at her life. She had a heavy job where she stood up for the rights of children whose parents were choosing to be criminals, or whose parents beat the children, or beat each other, or somehow did things against the law towards the children. She worked in a protective services division.

What I saw was that she kept everything confidential, and she took everything home with her. It had no way of leaving her body. So her head hurt, her shoulders hurt, her neck hurt, and her back hurt. But there was no "reason" a doctor could find. She carried migraine medicine and took it like it was breath mints.

I asked her if she could be disciplined to leave work at work. So on the drive home, I asked if she would be willing to ask all of the work problems (that she so valiantly solved during the day) to stay at work. Could she give herself space and freedom from those issues when she was at home? I said that the problems would be solved easier and faster if she came to work refreshed, rather than holding them in her body each night and weekend.

Even within an hour of our conversation, her head felt better. She saw how holding everything inside – truly nothing could leave, she was the "protector" of all those children and as a result, she was making herself ill. We looked at "would the children be served if she came to work fresh each day and didn't carry the burdens home every night" and we saw that they could be served even better, because she would be more brilliant in coming up with options for changes.

It was an interesting experience, seeing her hold all of the energy inside of her. I wonder what I am holding in my body today that if I released could change everything? And am I willing to be that fresh vessel each morning, clear of everyone else's judgments and expectations of me?

As a Writer

As a writer and an author, I am agreeing to be a target for judgment. One critic even said about my book "Happiness Quotations," that she didn't like it because it was too happy. That's so funny! I listen to critics, and I am always curious about what they are like with others. So sometimes I ask for a reality check. In the instance of the one less than five-star review about my book, I went and read all of the reviewer's other reviews. They were all critical and mean-spirited. So I was joyful. She was choosing to be unhappy, so even my happiness book could not be received by this specific critic.

If you've ever left your path due to a critical comment, I'd like to ask you to stop that right now. Just stop. You have to believe in you. Now, if you wish to be an opera singer and you've only sang rap music, it may take some time to train your voice differently. Or if you wish to rap and you've only played classical piano, you might be on a learning curve.

When you have a burning desire that is connected to your soul and the very being of you, give it some time to integrate into your waking reality.

Reality begins someplace else and then is created in the physical plane. So when you ask for a new reality, and release all judgment on it, it can fly in as if with wings. When you judge it or go back and forth about it, or choose to believe then not to believe, it isn't as quick to show up in the physical plane.

We live in a responsive universe. Millions of people and feelings and cells and energies are responding to you all the time. When you spend too much time hating yourself, you aren't spending time growing, expanding, creating, and living your dream.

And I use "hate" like all those words of doubt, memories of failures, past lifetimes where you never got it done, relationships that failed, any of that stuff that shows up when you are just about to break through to the next level of being.

When you get very, very close to the next level of being something might show up to test you. Like a very critical thought or a very big block. Look at it with curiosity. "I wonder what you are doing here big ugly thing I brought into my life? I wonder what it would take for you not to be here at all? I wonder what it would take if I woke up without you? Could I let you go? Could I release your power over me? What would that be like? What would that experience of being on the other side of this obstacle be like? Am I open to that? Yes, if I am a yes to that, what changes will I make today?

I love the concept of "we aren't going to change if we stay the same." I had a rather odd experience of assisting a not-for-profit organization with doubling its bike ride participants from 500 one year to 1000 the year I served in a marketing role. I remember meeting with the CEO and she said "we have to change. Or things won't."

It was that moment of an epiphany.

What will change?

What can I change?

What change can I be?

What judgment can I release?

Where can drama be released so it is not present in my life?

And now, what is possible in the world, when I am shining so bright everyone around me has to go get some new sunglasses?

Yes, that.

ERICA MARIE GLESSING

Erica Marie Glessing is a dreamer, a creative, a bright spirit who laughs easily and often. She is the CEO of Happy Publishing, joyful to have generated #1 bestselling author status for more than 115 authors to date. Who knows what she will be up to next!

Look for Erica here:

www.HappyPublishing.net
www.EricaGlessing.com,
on Facebook @happinessquotations,
and Twitter @ericaglessing.

THE END

CPSIA information can be obtained at www.ICGtesting.com
Printed in the USA
LVOW10s2210170316

479683LV00032B/781/P